KING ARTHUR AND
THE KNIGHTS OF
THE ROUND TABLE

KING ARTHUR AND THE KNIGHTS OF THE ROUND TABLE

Antonia Fraser

Orion

For Stella, Blanche, Atalanta and Thomas now

This edition published in Great Britain in 1993
by Orion Children's Books
A division of the Orion Publishing Group Ltd
Orion House
5 Upper St Martin's Lane
London WC2H 9EA

A catalogue record for this book is available from
the British Library

Typeset by Deltatype Ltd, Ellesmere Port
Printed in Great Britain by Clays Ltd, St Ives plc

ISBN 1 85881 003 5

CONTENTS

1

THE SON OF THE DRAGON

*I*t was midnight. In the mighty stronghold of Camelot a great king lay dying. Uther Pendragon's face was wasted, his eyes were glazed with sickness, and he had said nothing to his knights for many hours.

'So ends the rule of the Pendragons,' whispered one knight sadly to the other, 'for Uther Pendragon has no son to succeed him. Evil days will fall upon the west of Britain now, and we shall all be lost.' The Queen Igraine looked up from where she knelt at the bedside of the king and signed angrily to the knight to be silent. Abashed, the two knights bowed low, and stole out of the room on to the battlements, where they could talk unobserved. The cool night air fanned their hot faces.

'Uther Pendragon has been the greatest king in the west for many years,' said the first knight at length. 'It was Uther who first drove out the Saxon invaders, and repelled the dreadful pagan onslaughts. When I was a boy, no king was brave enough to resist them; but Uther's courage has set an example which other chieftains have dared to follow.'

'He was a great man,' agreed his companion. 'Many a time I have followed him into battle and seen his powerful lance terrorize the invaders. Other times I have watched him sweep all before him in the tournaments, and reflected that we shall not see his like again in Britain.' Suddenly the cry of women was heard in the inner room, disturbing the silence of the night. The two knights clutched each other.

'It is all over,' said one in a frightened voice. 'Let us return and pay our last respects to him, as he lies in death.' Scarcely had the two left the battlements, when a stealthy figure appeared round the buttress and beckoned to a companion muffled in a cloak.

'Is all prepared to seize the castle?' whispered the unknown.

'Down to the last man-at-arms,' came the gloating reply. 'This very night I shall be king in the place of Uther Pendragon. By foul means or fair I, Mordred, will sit upon the most powerful throne in Britain.' As he spoke the figure in the cloak swept back its draperies and revealed a face of extraordinary beauty – a skin of unearthly pallor and great dark eyes, surrounded by a thick mass of long black hair.

'Fear not, Mordred,' said the woman, 'for my magic has revealed to me that our plans will be successful.' She paused. 'We need have no further doubts were it not for the fact that –' and the woman broke off, as if afraid to continue.

'Well, Morgan Le Fay,' cried the man impatiently, 'what is there still to fear? Do not tantalize me with your hints.'

'My magic spells seem to reveal that Uther Pendragon has a son in hiding,' said Morgan Le Fay reluctantly. Mordred swore a terrible oath.

'It cannot be!' he exclaimed. 'Surely some rumour would have reached us of his existence before now. In any case, if there is an heir to the throne, why does he not come to his father's deathbed? No, Morgan Le Fay, your magic has led you astray this once. Uther Pendragon has no son. The queen only gave birth once and that child died of the fever.' Morgan Le Fay shrugged her shoulders. She said no more. Her mind went back to the time of the king's marriage, and the mysterious part which the wizard Merlin had played in bringing Uther and Igraine together. Had she not felt even then that there was something at the back of the wizard's kindness which only the king knew? Morgan Le Fay remembered the old country prophecy that the son of the dragon should prove the greatest king that Britain had ever known, and she shivered in her cloak. For 'the son of the dragon' could mean no other than the son of Uther Pendragon. However, she did not dare reveal her suspicions to Mordred, and followed him obediently from the battlements.

Little did the conspirators know that their talk had been overheard by an unseen witness, crouching in the shadow of the flag-tower. Out of the shadows stepped Merlin the wizard, mortal enemy of Morgan Le Fay and all her evil practices. The aged wizard leant on his stick and gazed after the treacherous pair.

'Morgan Le Fay suspects something,' he said aloud; 'I did not think her spells were strong enough to get so near the truth. But just now I read in her mind uneasy thoughts about the old prophecy concerning the "son of the dragon". I must act quickly to prevent my secret being discovered before the time is ripe.' The wizard descended a secret stairway which led from the battlements outside

3

the castle wall. Once free of the castle precincts, he mounted his horse and rode away towards the west.

As the wizard jogged along, he too cast his mind back to the marriage of Uther and Igraine. But unlike Morgan Le Fay, Merlin knew the full truth about that ill-fated marriage. He remembered Uther's desperate courtship of Igraine, the proud daughter of the Duke of Tintagel. The Cornish princess scorned to leave her rocky castle for the sake of the young king, who had as yet made no name for himself in battle. Haughtily she told him to return when he had extended his realm a little farther, and could offer her a worthier throne.

A lesser man would have been put off for ever by this high-handed treatment. But Uther was full of spirit and ambition; he vowed to tame the proud beauty and win her hand, no matter how long it took him. In all the years he fought the invaders, and acquired new lands by conquest or allegiance, he never lost sight of his ultimate goal – the hand of the Princess Igraine. However, when middle age overtook the king, and still Igraine remained obdurate, the king decided to enlist the help of his friend Merlin. Merlin listened with sympathy to Uther's predicament, and immediately offered to put his magic spells at his disposal. He even volunteered to fetch Igraine from Cornwall himself, if Uther would promise him something in return. The king was only too willing to promise the wizard anything he wanted, for the sake of Igraine. So Merlin went to Tintagel, and hypnotized Igraine into submission by the magic of his personality, which in those days no human being could resist. The high-spirited princess consented to follow the wizard docilely to Camelot, and there on the green grass before

4

the castle, Merlin put her hand in the king's.

That tender scene was one of his happiest memories. Then his thoughts passed on to the birth of Igraine's son, the child who was believed to have died of fever. It had been the height of summer when the queen gave birth to the baby Arthur. As she lay on her pillows, contentedly watching the child rocked in its cradle by her women, a shadow came between her and the light. Looking up, the queen saw Merlin watching her. Merlin still remembered her heart-rending cry when he took the child from its cradle; the mother's grief haunted him ten years later. But he steeled himself to ignore her. In vain the queen cried for her husband to arrest him and return the baby. When Uther ran forward and barred the wizard's way with his sword, Merlin brushed his blade aside.

'Let me pass, Uther,' he cried in a loud authoritative voice. 'Do you not remember your promise? You swore to grant me anything in the world if I would win the Princess Igraine for you. Now Igraine is your queen. Keep that oath, Uther, and let me take your son.' The sword dropped from Uther's numb fingers. He groped for words but none came. He could not believe that the wizard could be so cruel as to rob him of his only child. The queen's screams distracted him; the king rushed to help her. When he returned the wizard had vanished.

Merlin passed his hand over his brow, as if to wipe out the memory of that painful scene. Uther had never suspected what it cost Merlin to cause his friend such heartfelt agony. They had never referred to the incident again. Uther gave it out that the child had died of a fever, and ordered the courtiers not to mention the name of Arthur to the queen. On the surface Uther and Merlin

5

were as close friends as before. But the thought of Arthur lay between them. The old intimacy was gone.

Dwelling on the past, Merlin had arrived at a castle. The drawbridge was raised. The wizard took the bugle which hung from his saddle and blew it three times. In a few minutes, two young boys were racing towards him. A sturdy curly-headed boy reached him first, a yard ahead of his companion.

'Merlin!' panted the boy, 'it is good to see you. We have not had a visit from you for many months. I am an expert with the bow and arrow now, you know, and score a bull's-eye on the target every time.' The wizard patted his head affectionately.

'You have grown, Arthur,' he said.

'I am still taller,' cried the second boy proudly, as he puffed after Arthur. 'And I can shoot quite as straight as Arthur.'

'Greetings, Kay,' said the wizard with a smile. 'Is your father, Sir Hector, in the castle?' The two boys replied that Sir Hector was somewhere about his estates. They dragged the wizard off to judge a shooting competition by the mill-stream. The wizard watched Kay draw his bow and fire his arrow straight at an apple, balanced precariously on the rail of the bridge. Kay's arrow grazed the apple, and shook it on its perch; but Arthur's arrow cut the apple in half, so that the two halves fell into the mill-stream, and floated away. The wizard applauded heartily.

'It isn't fair,' said Kay crossly. 'His shot has wasted a good apple, but mine hit it without sending it into the stream. So mine was really the better shot. I deserve the prize.' The wizard remarked tactfully that they both deserved prizes, Arthur for his marksmanship, and Kay for his forethought. He drew two more luscious apples from his pocket and presented them to the boys. Munching contentedly, all three went up to the castle.

The first thing Merlin wanted to do was to have a private talk with Sir Hector about the future. Long ago, when he first brought the baby Arthur to the castle, he had confided the secret of his birth to Hector, who was an old comrade of Uther Pendragon. Hector had been charged to bring up the boy like his own son until the time was ripe for Arthur to claim his inheritance. So Kay and Arthur had been brought up to believe they were brothers. Hector had respected Merlin's trust and never breathed a word of Arthur's royal lineage to anyone.

But before Merlin could draw Hector aside, the knight seized the wizard's arm and whispered: 'I must speak with you. Uther Pendragon is dead and Mordred has usurped the throne.' Merlin nodded. 'We must talk,' he replied. 'Tell the boys to groom down their horses.' As Kay and Arthur raced off to the stables, Merlin and Hector started to plan the future.

'First of all, Hector, I must impress upon you that the time has not yet come for Arthur to assume the crown which is rightfully his,' began the wizard. Hector's face fell. He had imagined a long regency, with himself guiding the hand of the young king. 'The state of Britain is too turbulent for a regent,' continued Merlin, who had guessed his thoughts. 'Arthur must wait until his eighteenth birthday and then win his throne by the sword. The immediate problem is how to keep him out of the hands of Mordred. I have a feeling in my bones that Morgan Le Fay suspects the existence of Uther's son.'

MORDRED STRIKES

A violent bray of trumpets at the gates distracted them. Sir Hector sent his squire to find out what the noise meant. The news was brought back that a party of men-at-arms were outside, with instructions from the new King Mordred to search the castle. Hector and Merlin exchanged looks. Mordred had caught them off their guard by acting so quickly.

'What insolence!' exclaimed Sir Hector. 'How dare Mordred claim the right to search my castle!' The wizard bent forward and whispered in his ear, 'Whatever your feelings, don't try to stop them. If we let them search and find nothing, they will go away and never come back. If we try and keep them out, Mordred himself will come back with an army and smoke you out of your stronghold. For God's sake, don't arouse their suspicions.' Controlling himself with an effort, Sir Hector ordered the soldiers to be admitted. He received them with cold courtesy. The sergeant produced his warrant from the king.

'King Mordred wants a full tally of the inhabitants of every castle,' said the fellow. 'From the highest to the lowest – and the oldest to the youngest. Order all your household to assemble here, that we may check them for the king.' Merlin did not miss the significance of the word 'youngest'. So it *was* the boy they were after. Morgan Le Fay would have worked out the age of Uther Pendragon's son. She must have suggested the tally to Mordred, as a neat way of discovering the boy prince's hiding-place. Merlin smiled grimly; Morgan Le Fay was a more dangerous enemy than he had supposed. It never did to underestimate a woman who was half a witch. In the

8

hours which had passed since the king's death she must have guessed the truth about Arthur's supposed death, and organized the check. He would have to pay more attention to Morgan Le Fay in the future!

Merlin gave a faint wink at Sir Hector.

'It would be as well if I summoned the ostlers and grooms from the stables,' he said, 'for they will not hear your bugle from here.' Sir Hector nodded, and the wizard hobbled out. The sergeant tapped his foot impatiently on the marble floor, as serving women, men-at-arms, pantry boys and kitchen maids came into the hall in frightened groups. They huddled together, overawed by the king's soldiers.

At length Merlin led in a body of men, who had evidently come straight from the stables, for straw still stuck to their boots. Kay sidled in beside the wizard. But there was no sign of Arthur. Sir Hector wondered where the wizard had hidden the boy – surely he must realize that the soldiers would comb every inch of the grounds. Then he counted the stable-boys – one, two, three, four . . . five, six! . . . Sir Hector knew perfectly well that there were only five boys in his stable. He realized that Merlin had taken the desperate course of dirtying Arthur's face and dressing him up in the ragged clothes of the other stable-boys.

The sergeant made only a perfunctory check on the grown-up members of the household. His eyes narrowed when he saw the array of boys. Watching him closely, Sir Hector saw him smile in anticipation, as if he had been given orders by the king to cope with this situation. The sergeant pulled Kay before him and stared into the boy's defiant face.

'What is your name, my lad?' he asked. 'And whose son are you?'

'Kay is my name and Sir Hector is my father.' Kay looked so like his father that the sergeant was satisfied. He left Kay and turned to the rank of stable-boys. The sergeant walked up and down, peering into each face in turn. Sir Hector held his breath. The blood royal could not help showing in the way Arthur held himself; his bearing, the very boldness of his behaviour proclaimed him to be of higher rank than the rest of the boys. Sure enough, the sergeant returned to Arthur at the end of his scrutiny. He subjected him to another searching stare.

'Roll up your sleeve, boy.' The sergeant spat out the words. Blind panic possessed Sir Hector. How *could* they have forgotten the mark of the dragon, the ineradicable brand on Arthur's arm, which had been tattooed on him at birth as the son of the king? It looked as if the game was up. Sir Hector's hand tightened on his sword; he was prepared to defend the young prince to the death.

Slowly Arthur rolled up his sleeve. The mark of the dragon showed livid on his arm. With a cry of triumph, the sergeant pounced on him and drew him forth from the rank of boys.

'We've got him,' he bellowed, 'the son of the dragon himself, the lost son of Uther whom we have been sent to find. Bind him, men, so that we may bear him before King Mordred.' Merlin's clear voice cut through the confusion which followed, with Arthur kicking and struggling, Kay cutting at the sergeant with his miniature sword, and Sir Hector shouting to his men to bar the entrance and prevent the soldiers from leaving.

'One moment, Sergeant,' said Merlin, 'are you quite sure you are not making a very stupid mistake?'

'Sure enough,' replied the sergeant with a rough laugh. 'We were told to look for the lad with the dragon mark, and it seems we have found him.'

'Then I suggest you examine the rest of the stable-boys,' said Merlin calmly. In silence the sergeant released Arthur and gazed at the bared arms of the five other stable-boys. On each one the mark of the dragon stood out livid on the white flesh!

'Perhaps I should have warned you that this morning Sir Hector ordered all his stable-boys to be tattooed with the mark of the dragon, in memory of the dead king,' said Merlin smoothly. Not trusting himself to speak, Sir Hector simply nodded. The sergeant's face flushed with anger. He realized that he had been made to look a fool in front of all his men, and that Sir Hector would probably report his mistake to the king. Standing stiffly to attention, he bowed to the knight and to the wizard.

'A regrettable error,' he said. 'I shall take my leave of you.' The sergeant hesitated. He was clearly on the verge of adding something.

'I see no reason why this unfortunate incident should ever get to the ears of the king,' put in Merlin diplomatically. The sergeant's relief was obvious. He signalled to his men and left the castle, to seek the son of the dragon elsewhere.

As the door clanged to behind him, Sir Hector turned to Merlin and burst out: 'But how did it happen? How on earth did you manage it?'

'Magic has its uses, my dear Sir Hector,' replied Merlin complacently. 'We wizards do not spend our whole time gazing into the future, you know. We can be men of action when it suits us.' The wizard hummed a little tune of satisfaction, and allowed himself to be congratulated all round on his cleverness. The five stable-boys examined their bare arms in wonder, where only a moment ago the mark of the dragon had stood out on the flesh. Only Arthur drew a little apart and said nothing.

'The son of the dragon,' he mused. 'What does that mean? What strange future is in store for me?'

2

THE SWORD IN THE STONE

*W*hatever the future had in store for Arthur, the next few years were uneventful enough. King Mordred left Sir Hector in peace in his castle. The two boys grew to manhood, and never suspected the truth about Arthur's royal birth. Rumours of Mordred's misdeeds reached Sir Hector from time to time; but the old knight only shook his grey head in sorrow and sighed for the days of Uther Pendragon. However, when he learned that Mordred had made a treaty with the Saxons, allowing them certain lands in the south, his indignation burst out.

'Oh, craven king!' he shouted, storming up and down the great hall. 'Unworthy to bear the crown which Uther Pendragon once wore! That I should live to hear of my sovereign feasting with the Saxons, those pagan enemies of Christ.'

'When I am old enough I shall fight the Saxons,' said Arthur boldly. 'I shall raise a band of warriors against them.'

'So shall I,' chimed in Kay. 'I shall raise a bigger band than Arthur.'

'There's my brave lads,' said the old knight. 'At least that's a good omen for the future,' he added under his breath. 'We may one day have a king worthy of his salt.'

A year later, Merlin paid one of his rare visits to the castle. He brought word to Sir Hector that Mordred had ordered a tournament on the feast of Pentecost, at which the Saxon chiefs were to be guests of honour. The old knight turned purple in the face with rage, and vowed that neither he nor his two boys would set foot in Camelot while the Saxons were there.

'Feeling is running high against Mordred,' said the wizard significantly. 'If a new leader were to appear at Pentecost, I have no doubt that he would get a good deal of support.' Sir Hector gazed at Merlin. The wizard nodded. 'The time is ripe, Hector,' was all he said. The knight immediately withdrew all objections. He bade the boys polish their armour and groom their horses, for they were about to take part in their first tournament at Camelot itself. Arthur and Kay were in a state of high excitement. When the day itself arrived, of course Arthur and Kay had got nothing ready. They had been far too busy practising in the meadows. Both of them had to fling on their armour all askew, for which they got a severe lecture from Sir Hector.

'Knights!' he said scornfully, as they were entering Camelot three abreast. 'Fine knights you two would make. Your helmets are crooked, your shields need a good lick of paint, and your breastplates need polishing. As for your swords! Look at Arthur's hilt, just about as bright as a foggy day.' Kay turned slightly pale when his father mentioned his sword, but he said nothing. Arthur was too busy gazing round him at the busy scene to notice. Pennants waved gaily in the breeze, horses neighed and whinnied, knights in heavy armour with noble crests on their shields called for a passage through the crowd. Everywhere was bustle and excitement. Arthur was so happy. He felt that all his life had been leading up to this moment.

In the royal pavilion, facing the lists, sat the King Mordred. He was scowling at his queen, Morgan Le Fay. Sir Hector could see that they were quarrelling. Could Morgan Le Fay have counselled him against inviting the Saxons? She was making no effort to entertain the Saxon chief on her right. The common people outside the barricades were shouting insults at the Saxons, and saying openly that a man who sat at table with heathens was not fit to be a king.

'Saxons should be handled at the point of the sword,' said one fellow loudly in Arthur's hearing, 'not with the velvet gloves which our *brave* King Mordred uses.' The fellow put a wealth of sarcasm into the word 'brave'. Arthur had no time to hear more, for the first rounds of sword-play were beginning. As he was making his way into the lists, Kay suddenly tugged at his arm. His face was white.

'Arthur,' he whispered, 'you must help me. In all the confusion I have left my sword behind, and unless you do something, I shall not be able to take part in the tournament.' Arthur did not hesitate. He thrust his own sword into Kay's hand, and without waiting for Kay to thank him, slipped off into the crowd, saying that he would find one for himself. He did not want to steal one, and he had no money to buy one. Arthur felt rather dismayed when he reflected how blithely he had handed over his own sword to Kay. Suddenly –

'What a stroke of luck!' exclaimed Arthur, 'someone

has left a sword stuck in this stone. I can borrow it for the tournament, and return it later.' His wanderings had brought him to the green grass outside the cathedral. A huge boulder lay on the verge of the grass. In its centre was plunged a sword, stuck so deeply into the stone that only the hilt showed. Some lettering ran round the base of the stone, but Arthur had no time to waste reading it. In any case, it probably said it was forbidden to touch the sword, and the less he knew about that the better. So he grasped the hilt firmly in both his hands and tugged hard at the sword. To his surprise it came out of the stone as easily as if it had been stuck in butter. Quite a crowd watched Arthur perform his feat. Had he paid more attention to them, he might have seen the expressions of fear and astonishment on their faces. But Arthur was chiefly concerned to get back to the tournament as quickly as possible.

Arthur was just in time to see Kay defeated in a brisk fight with a much older squire. The boy defended himself ably, and Sir Hector felt proud of him. Arthur rushed into the lists, and challenged the nearest swordsman. He wielded his sword like a full-grown man experienced in a dozen fights. All his opponents fell before Arthur. Arthur was the unvanquished hero of the tournament.

All this time a steady murmur was rising in the crowd. At first it was no more than the wordless sound of many people whispering together; but gradually the words became clearer. Icy hands clutched at the heart of Mordred. What were they saying down there behind the barricades, the people who had never loved him, the people who called him 'the craven king'?

'The sword in the stone!' he heard the crowd say – they

were shouting in unison: 'The boy has drawn the sword from the stone.' Mordred turned to Morgan Le Fay. She had risen from her seat, and was gazing wildly round her.

'It has happened,' she cried. 'What I have feared all these years has happened. The son of the dragon has come to turn you off your throne. He has drawn the sword from the stone, and with it he will surely slay you, Mordred.'

'Peace, woman,' shouted Mordred. 'You will ruin us all with your doleful prophecies. What is the sword in the stone to me? Some magic hocus-pocus of Merlin's, I have no doubt. I see no armed knight, no ranks of mailed soldiers in front of me. What can a boy, and a few ruffians do against me and my guards?'

But Mordred was only blustering to keep his spirits up. Was it only a year ago that this strange apparition had been found in the cathedral close after a night of thunder and lightning? The enormous stone was engraved round its base with these words:

'Only the true king can draw the sword from the stone.' When Mordred read this, he immediately seized the hilt in his huge hands and pulled at it with all his might. He strained and sweated, but the sword would not move. It was as immovable as the cathedral itself. The crowd groaned, and hissed Mordred when he failed. He heard the tell-tale whispers:

'Mordred is not the true king. Mordred cannot draw the sword from the stone,' but he pretended not to understand them.

Now a boy, stamped with the unmistakable look of a Pendragon, confronted him at the head of the very people who had hissed him. Arthur's face was set, and he looked older than his eighteen years. His sleeve had fallen back;

and on his arm the mark of the dragon stood out so forcibly that Mordred's fascinated gaze was drawn to it as by a magnet. In his heart of hearts, Mordred, like Morgan Le Fay, knew the hour of reckoning had come. But if Mordred was cruel, he at last found bravery, with the courage of an animal at bay. He did not cringe before Arthur, nor beg for mercy, nor seek to escape through the back of the royal box. Grimly, he bade his guards draw weapons and stand close. As the crowd approached Mordred, it divided to let Arthur lead the procession. Arthur looked strangely young and frail in contrast to the mighty Mordred. But he did not falter.

'Prepare to do battle for your throne, Mordred!' he shouted, 'for I am Arthur Pendragon, come to claim the crown which belonged to my father.' A great cheer went up from his followers as he declared himself. Next to Arthur, Mordred saw the watchful figure of the wizard Merlin, supporting his protégé in his critical hour. At the sight of Merlin, a lot of things were clear to Mordred. So Uther's son really had survived! Morgan Le Fay had been right to suspect that the Pendragons had not died out with Uther. Mordred cursed himself for having disregarded her warnings. But it was too late for regrets now. With a war-cry, he leapt down from the pavilion, and rushed at Arthur with drawn sword. The boy did not flinch from this ferocious attack. He defended himself vigorously against Mordred. While Mordred's enemies hacked at the hated guards, and revenged themselves on the Saxon chiefs, the false king and the young prince fought a great duel with the throne as a prize. The frightened spectators held their breath to see the blows which Mordred dealt the stripling Arthur – but Arthur was a match for them. Again and again he survived a great thrust of Mordred's sword, and hit out boldly at Mordred. At last Mordred seemed to weaken. He stepped back a pace before Arthur's onslaught, faltered, slipped, his guard dropped for a split second, and Arthur was upon him.

So perished Mordred at the hand of Arthur. No one ever deserved to die more than this cruel king. He had usurped the crown, and then degraded it by his cowardice. Amid the cheers of the crowd, and many of the knights who had secretly loathed Mordred, Merlin acclaimed Arthur as the new king. Arthur's mother, Queen Igraine, embraced her long-lost son with cries of joy. Once more a Pendragon sat upon the throne!

But what of Morgan Le Fay? When she saw her husband slain, the witch queen crept away unseen and escaped from Camelot. If Arthur had pursued and slain her, as he slew her husband, much bloodshed and sorrow in the future might have been avoided!

3

EXCALIBUR

'A beardless boy on the throne of Mordred! That's the best joke I have heard this year,' said King Leodegrance of Cameliard, when he heard the news of Arthur's accession. King Mark of Cornwall laughed out loud when he received the scroll summoning him to Arthur's coronation. King Pellenore did not even bother to read it. All over Britain powerful barons mocked at the idea of taking an oath of loyalty to a boy of eighteen, as yet untried in battle.

'They laugh at me now,' said Arthur, when the news of their refusal was brought to him. 'But I swear there will come a day when they crawl before me and beg for my assistance.' He refused to allow these insolent messages to interrupt the preparations for his coronation. The story of the sword which had been drawn from the stone was told and retold in castles and manorhouses all over the country. Enough loyal knights set out for Camelot for there to be a brave display of chivalry on Arthur's coronation day. The king hid his chagrin at the absence of the powerful lords. He ordered there to be banquets and tournaments without ceasing for thirty days to celebrate the event. The miserly reign of Mordred was over! No expense was spared in the lavish and magnificent arrangements.

'My courts and my knights will one day be the most famous in Britain,' Arthur told Merlin proudly, 'and I want my coronation day to be remembered for a hundred years. What do I care if King Leodegrance and King Mark scorn me? Knights and squires are flocking into Camelot by every gate. If I win the affection of the people, I shall have a powerful weapon against these proud rebellious kings.'

When Arthur had taken the oath in the cathedral, swearing to serve God and rule his people justly all his life, the archbishop placed the crown on his head. In turn, his vassals knelt before him and took the oath of allegiance. They placed their hands between his, and promised to be faithful to him in peace and in war.

Once the coronation ceremony was over, and Arthur had been acclaimed by the people of Camelot, it was time for the tournament to begin. It was Arthur himself, mounted on a fine charger, who was the first to ride up and down the lists and challenge all comers. His foster-brother Kay took up the challenge eagerly.

'It would be a fine thing if I could unseat Arthur and so win my spurs today,' he thought. But Arthur was more than a match for Kay: he belaboured Kay and toppled him off his horse. Kay leapt cheerfully to his feet.

'Well done, Arthur,' he cried, showing that he bore no resentment for defeat. 'Now it is time for the king to retire to his royal pavilion and leave the field to his subjects. What is the prize for the winner of this tournament?'

'A knighthood! By my royal oath, I swear to knight the winner.' So saying, Arthur rode off to his pavilion and took his seat there. Inwardly, he felt rather sad at having to leave the fighting; but it was all part of the mixed joy and sadness of being a king. In future he would have to realize that he could not joust and tilt freely, as Kay could. He had a responsibility to his people.

KAY MEETS DISASTER

Kay was anxious to win his spurs, so all day he fought like a man inspired. Towards the end of the tournament his sword arm was weary and his armour showed several fearful rents, but he was still undefeated. Only one other knight could say the same. This was an unknown knight, whose shield bore no crest. Kay did not recognize his horse or his armour. It occurred to him that this might be a spy sent by Pellenore or Mark of Cornwall; he resolved to challenge the Unknown in the last round of the tournament and unmask him.

The Unknown would not put up his visor to answer Kay's challenge. His voice was muffled and soft as he replied:

'I have waited all day to fight with you, Kay, brother of Arthur, for I think you are an opponent worthy of my steel.' With these words the Unknown spurred his horse and galloped forward. Kay galloped towards the Unknown at full speed, but although he dealt the Unknown a mighty blow with his lance, which would have rocked a lesser man in the saddle, his new opponent scarcely seemed to feel it.

Kay's second charge was even more unsuccessful, for the Unknown's lance penetrated one of the rents in his armour and pierced his leg. The pain made Kay faint and dizzy, but he set his teeth and aimed a blow wildly back at his enemy. At the third charge Kay could no longer survive the savage onslaught, and at the impact of the Unknown's fierce blows, he tottered in the saddle and tumbled heavily to the ground.

A groan went up from the crowd, for Kay was popular, and nothing was known about the stranger. Arthur himself hated to see his foster-brother bite the dust at the hand of an anonymous knight. But he had a duty to fulfil. He faced the Unknown graciously and asked him to put up his visor.

The face which confronted him belonged to no spy from Leodegrance or Pellenore. He saw a young and dazzlingly handsome man, scarcely older than himself, who smiled frankly at the king.

'Come, admit that you expected someone much older,' said the Unknown, laughing, 'or a monster, or perhaps King Leodegrance of Cameliard himself. But I have no high position or formidable reputation. I am simply a young soldier of fortune, who has come to your court, Arthur Pendragon, because the idea of a gallant young king facing his enemies on all sides appealed to me. I am Lancelot, and I lay my sword at your service.' This honest speech pleased Arthur. He had need of men like this, if he was going to win back the lands which Mordred had sacrificed to the Saxons! Without hesitation he accepted Lancelot's offer of service, and bade him kneel to receive the knighthood which was the prize of the tournament. Thus Sir Lancelot was the first knight whom Arthur created in his reign. The second was naturally Sir Kay, for Arthur had no desire to annoy his touchy foster-brother by preferring a stranger to him. In spite of his

defeat of the tournament, Kay received the prized acco-
lade, with the flat of Arthur's sword.

THE TREACHERY OF KING PELLENORE

Scarcely were the thirty days of feasting over, than grave
news was brought to the king. An exhausted messenger,
dusty from a long and hectic ride, and blood-stained from
a wound in the arm, flung himself at the king's feet.

'My liege, save us from the Saxons!' he panted. 'The
south of Britain groans under the heel of the invader, and
we shall all die of starvation if we survive massacre.' Sir
Kay bent down and examined the body stretched at
Arthur's feet. His eyes narrowed when he saw the crest on
the fellow's jerkin.

'This is one of Pellenore's men,' he said in Arthur's ear.
'I know that crest only too well. Have a care, Arthur, for I
suspect a trap.' Arthur raised the man to his knees. There
was no doubt that he was genuinely exhausted by a long
ride, and weakened by a wound. But why should
Pellenore's men come to Arthur for help? Arthur decided
that a surprise attack would help him get the truth.

'Miserable spy!' he said angrily. 'Why do you come to
me with this lying tale! I can see that you are one of
Pellenore's ruffians. Pellenore can look after his own
lands, since he will not take the oath of allegiance to me. A
day or two in my dungeons will teach you to try and trap
Arthur Pendragon.' The man groaned.

'My liege,' he said faintly. 'Have mercy on me. It is true
I am one of Pellenore's vassals – or rather I was. But that
base king is even now making a treaty with the invaders
which will give them all the lands they want in the south.

24

Now you see why I cannot appeal to Pellenore for help.'
Arthur's face darkened in anger. So Pellenore, like
Mordred, was playing the British chiefs false, by making
private arrangements with the Saxons! It was time to put
an end to this state of affairs, and depose Pellenore from
the throne which he occupied so unworthily.

He ordered the heralds to blow their trumpets from the
battlements. It was war! A week later, with head held
high, Arthur rode out from Camelot on a magnificent
white horse at the head of his men. It was the first time he
had led his people in battle, and he prayed that he might
prove a leader worthy of them. Along the road, the burnt
hayricks and ruined buildings testified to the ruthless
Saxon raids and the treachery of Pellenore. Old men and
women crouched in the ditches, clutching the few posses-
sions which were left to them. Children wept, and clung to
their mothers' skirts. Some of those who recognized
Arthur, cried out with joy, and acclaimed him as the
saviour of their country. The young king's heart leapt to
hear their cries.

'I *have* won the affection of the people,' he thought.
'Now I must win their admiration by fighting like a king.'

They were now deep in the heart of Pellenore's country.
Arthur took Lancelot's advice, and decided to march on
Pellenore's castle from two sides. Lancelot, with fifty of
the boldest knights, was to attack from the west. Arthur
was to lead the main body of the army by the front road.
From his battlements, Pellenore watched them approach.
Once again he refused to take 'the boy king', as he
derisively called him, seriously. It was a mistake which
was to cost him dear. He took no particular trouble with
the defences of the castle. He did not even bother to send

word warning his allies the Saxons, who were encamped over the hill, out of sight of the approaching army. Pellenore idled away the hours in his great hall, composing songs in honour of his victory over Arthur. The fact that this victory had not yet happened did not worry Pellenore at all.

The cries of the Saxons, and clash of arms took Pellenore completely by surprise. Rushing to the window, he saw that his allies, the so-called terror of the south, were being put to the sword by the despised 'boy king'! The invaders had no time to make plans before Arthur and his army were upon them. In a panic, the Saxons thought only of flight and the safety of their ships. Pellenore could see the scurrying forms of the leaders heading for the coast. Behind them raced Arthur, brandishing his sword and decimating their broken ranks.

'Man the walls!' shouted King Pellenore. 'We have no time to lose, if we are to survive this onslaught. I can see that Arthur Pendragon is a general to be reckoned with.'

'My liege,' said the king's squire apologetically, 'we have scarcely a fighting force in the castle. Most of the best men were given leave to go back to their homes, after the treaty with the Saxons.' Pellenore frowned. It was too true. After a moment he smiled. If he could not save himself by fair means, then he would try foul. He sent for his chief herald.

An hour later, Arthur, encamped outside the castle of Pellenore, received a message from the king. It was extremely moderate and conciliating, unlike the insolent messages which he had sent to Arthur at his coronation. Pellenore suggested that the best way for the kings to settle their differences was by private combat. Thus much unnecessary bloodshed could be avoided. Pellenore appealed to Arthur's good sense and statesmanship. It was a subtle appeal: for Arthur was flattered by the implication that he was old enough to think other methods of settling squabbles rather crude. He had no reason to doubt Pellenore's good intentions. Gladly he accepted the challenge and, leaving his men at a distance, he rode forth to meet Pellenore alone.

He found the rebel king sitting proudly astride his charger at the foot of the castle. Arther felt a moment's doubt, when he saw how close the ranks of Pellenore's knights stood, and he remembered how far off he had left his own army. However, he rode forward confidently to meet Pellenore's challenge. The fight between the two kings was long and bitter; in the course of it Arthur sustained two deep wounds, and Pellenore himself was wounded in the shoulder by Arthur's spear. But Arthur managed to hold his own, until the very moment when the black-hearted Pellenore gave a secret signal, and the ranks of his knights plunged forward to overwhelm the young king. In the first moment of this treacherous attack, Arthur felt the strong sword which he had drawn from the stone splinter into a thousand pieces: then he was dragged from his horse, and hurled to the ground by a screaming mob of swordsmen. In the general mêlée, what chance did Arthur stand, alone against so many enemies? He had given himself up for lost, when suddenly the blows ceased, and his assailants turned to defend themselves against a new attack. Arthur had not the strength to pick himself off the ground, for he was wounded in every limb, and his armour had been torn from him: nevertheless, from the ground, he could see to his joy Sir Lancelot and his fifty men striking blow upon blow against Pellenore and his false knights! Later Arthur learned that Lancelot had come upon the scene just in time to see the king fall before the treacherous charge of Pellenore's men, and had come at full gallop to rescue his liege lord. Even so he had only managed by a miracle to rescue Arthur from death.

The fight between Sir Lancelot and King Pellenore was short and bloody: in a few moments the evil king lay on the ground, pierced to the heart – a fitting end for one who had broken the sacred rules of chivalry. Sir Lancelot himself bore the wounded king back to his own lines, and saw to it that Arthur's wounds were tended. Meanwhile Pellenore's followers, seeing their master slain, surrendered to Sir Lancelot, and forswore the Saxon alliance. The drawbridge was lowered, and Arthur carried inside at the head of his men.

The Lady of the Lake

It was many weeks before Arthur's wounds were fully healed: and during his convalescence, the king was often worried by the fact that the sword which he had drawn from the stone had been broken in the charge of the rebels. It seemed an evil omen. When the day came for him to mount his horse again and return to Camelot at the head of the army, his heart was heavy: at his side the borrowed sword hung in the borrowed scabbard, a perpetual reminder of his loss. Suddenly the wizard Merlin appeared at Arthur's side, one of the silent mysterious appearances which he loved to make.

'Tell Sir Lancelot to lead your men back to Camelot, my lord,' said Merlin in Arthur's ear. 'Then follow me alone, and I will lead you where you will find another sword, mightier than the one which was broken in battle with the treacherous hosts of Pellenore.' Arthur needed no second invitation. A swift command to Lancelot, and he was ready and willing to follow the wizard.

Merlin took him on a long journey. The paths they took were lonely and their way seemed to lie through many waste places. They passed through great forests without meeting a single traveller. Arthur suspected that the wizard was deliberately leading him by a winding route to prevent him remembering the way. When the wizard swore him to an oath of secrecy, Arthur replied that there was no need, because never in his life would he find such a tortuous route again.

'Yet you are destined to find this path once more during your lifetime,' replied Merlin. 'At the end of your life. I have seen it written in your fate.' Then he pointed ahead of him. What strange and wonderful sight was this? A great lake, like a huge looking-glass, stretched out as far as the eye could see. There was not a human being to be seen. No birds sang. No animals scampered across their path. Thick rushes fringed the edge of the lake where a solitary rowing-boat was drawn up. But this was not the sight which made Arthur hold his breath in fear and amazement: for out of the middle of the lake itself, extended an arm, clothed in a white sleeve, and grasping the hilt of a sword! Where there should have been a shoulder, the arm disappeared into the bosom of the lake. Arthur crossed himself.

'What trick of the devil is this, Merlin?' he asked roughly.

'This is no trick of the devil,' replied the wizard. 'The

Lady of the Lake herself is offering you the most powerful sword in Britain – Excalibur itself. The history of Excalibur is as old as the history of Britain; no one knows where that magic weapon first was forged, for the Lady of the Lake preserves her secret. But every century or so, she lends it to a favoured mortal. Take it, Arthur, for it is yours during your lifetime!' Without hesitation, the young king stepped into the rowing-boat and rowed speedily towards the white arm which glimmered in the middle of the lake. His imagination was fired by the thought of this powerful weapon, which would replace the sword drawn from the stone. When he reached the arm, he drew the sword gently from its grasp. Immediately the arm sank below the waves, and however hard he looked, Arthur could not see anything below the surface of the water. Thoughtfully, he rowed back to Merlin and showed him the sword.

'See to it that you are worthy of this famous blade,' said the wizard. 'Also, see to it that you guard the scabbard well. It is said to have magic powers, which protect the wearer from wounds.'

Arther felt most grateful towards the aged wizard for having brought him to this lonely place and helping him obtain the sword Excalibur. He thanked him from his heart; but the wizard disclaimed his thanks, and explained that he had acted on the instructions of the Lady of the Lake herself, who had wished to repay an old debt of gratitude to his father, Uther Pendragon. Arthur discovered that there were two inscriptions, one on each side of the blade: 'Keep me' and 'Cast me away'. He asked the wizard laughingly whether he should immediately cast the blade back into the lake; the wizard did not smile.

'The time has not yet come to cast away Excalibur,' he replied gravely. 'But when you feel the hour of your death is upon you, make your way back to this lake, and give back Excalibur to the Lady of the Lake.'

'I swear it,' said the king. But the hour of his death seemed a long way off to Arthur, and now that he had got a new sword he was impatient to return to Camelot. Bidding a hasty good-bye to the wizard, he leapt on his horse, and set off at a gallop back through the forest. Merlin watched him go with foreboding. He feared that the young king would meet some strange adventures before he reached Camelot: for the wizard's spells had warned him that Queen Morgan Le Fay was already plotting to overthrow Arthur. However, Arthur had not waited to hear his advice, and somewhat hurt, Merlin decided to let him go his own way and learn by his own mistakes.

Arthur Falls into a Trap

'I am the finest king in Britain now,' thought Arthur conceitedly, as he rode along. 'I have defeated the Saxons, vanquished King Pellenore – well, perhaps Lancelot did help a little, but it was in fact me who beat him – and now I have got Excalibur.' Arthur whistled a song of triumph to himself. But his pride was soon to have a fall.

A young girl, in a state of great distress, stopped him by the wayside and begged for his assistance. Arthur gallantly promised to help her. Perhaps if he had thought back to treachery of King Pellenore, which had fooled him, he might have been more wary now. But Arthur was convinced that no one could teach him anything. He hoisted the girl on to his horse and rode with her back to her house. He listened to the tale which she poured into his sympathetic ear. It was a confused story of a wicked stepmother and a lost inheritance, which Arthur had some difficulty in unravelling. Several times the girl even seemed to condradict herself, but Arthur put this down to her distress. He vowed to help her recover her inheritance, even if it meant fighting every stepfather in Britain single-handed. The girl was profuse in her gratitude, and suggested that Arthur should have a meal before setting out to brave her stepfather in his castle. The day had been long, and Arthur felt weary. He saw no objection to some bread and a glass of mead to refresh himself: yet the look of sly satisfaction on the girl's face should have warned him against drinking out of the goblet which she gave him. Sleep overcame Arthur as soon as he had drained the goblet. No sooner had his eyelids closed, than the innocent-looking girl underwent an amazing transformation. In a few moments the girl Arthur met had disappeared, and Morgan Le Fay herself stood there in her place, smiling cruelly over the helpless form of the king. Morgan Le Fay's arts enabled her to disguise herself in various ways without difficulty; and she had adopted the youthful appearance of a country girl in order to lure Arthur into her power. Without losing a moment, she seized the scabbard of Excalibur, and thrusting it under her cloak, stole silently away, leaving Arthur to sleep off the effects of the drug she had given him. It was several hours before Arthur stirred and woke. His head ached abominably, and he had no recollection of how he had come to lie in this deserted house. Dragging himself painfully to his feet, he made his way out, and straight to his horse.

As he rode towards Camelot, memory came back to him slowly. Arthur groaned in horror as he realized that he had been drugged and duped and, worse still, robbed – for Excalibur was now roped to his side by a common cord, and the magic scabbard was gone.

'Morgan Le Fay,' he thought. 'It must have been her plan to steal the scabbard, and so leave me vulnerable to the wounds of my enemies.' The king cursed himself for having neglected the advice of Merlin, and vowed to pay more attention to the wizard's warnings in future. He was also puzzled why Morgan Le Fay, having taken the scabbard, left the sword. The ways of magic were strange and mysterious to him and he did not know that the Lady of the Lake was actually the most powerful witch in Britain; her magic was considerably stronger than that of Queen Morgan Le Fay, who was half-witch and half-woman. It would need all Morgan Le Fay's most deep-laid plots to steal the famous sword Excalibur, as future events were to prove. In the meantime the witch queen had succeeded in half her plan to overthrow Arthur – she had stolen the scabbard and made sure that he could be wounded and killed like other mortals.

THE FOUNDING OF THE ROUND TABLE

'Camelot needs a queen!' Now the fatal words were out, and Sir Lancelot waited for an explosion of anger from Arthur. But to his surprise the king said nothing at all. He played with his beard thoughtfully and gazed out of the window. Sir Lancelot mopped his forehead with relief. In the five years he had served Arthur, he had never had a more delicate task to perform than explaining to the king that his knights thought he ought to marry. Lancelot, the hero of a hundred battles, the scourge of the Saxons, the peril of the wicked, thought twice before approaching Arthur with this message.

With the passing years, the boy who drew the sword from the stone had grown into a vigorous man. Princes and chieftains were now only too glad to bow before Arthur Pendragon. Knights flocked to Camelot, attracted by stories of the many fine adventures to be had there. The Saxons had been driven back. The rebel kings no longer dared send insolent messages to Arthur.

But although Arthur's court was famous for its tournaments, and its military strength, the manners of Arthur's knights were rude and boisterous. The king was rumoured to dislike all women (a rumour which arose out of his experience with the girl who stole his scabbard, and turned out to be Morgan Le Fay). There were no beautiful and gracious ladies at the court, but only flirtatious girls who plagued the life out of Lancelot and the other knights.

It was Lancelot who put the general feeling into words. 'If we had a queen to set us a good example, we might be as famous for our chivalry as we are for our victories.' Everyone laughed at Lancelot; for if ever there was a ladies' man, it was him. His good looks caused havoc in the heart of any girl who saw him. Lancelot had a way with him which all the other knights envied. But Lancelot refused to be teased out of his opinion.

'Who knows,' he said laughingly. 'If Arthur set me a good example by marrying, I might decide to settle down myself.' With these prophetic words, Lancelot persuaded the knights to accept his point of view. Now came the difficult problem of telling Arthur. To Lancelot's horror, he was unanimously selected for this task. Everyone made haste to point out that Lancelot had suggested the idea, and was therefore the proper person to tell Arthur. Lancelot cursed himself for ever having raised it, and went off to look for the king, with a sinking feeling.

But Arthur listened to Lancelot in silence.

'You were right to tell me about this,' he said at length. 'It is true that Camelot needs a queen. I have thought so for some time. You can tell the court that I hope to be married by Michaelmas.' Sir Lancelot was dumbfounded. He had never expected to be received like this. The best he had hoped for was a grudging acquiescence or a muttered 'We'll see'. He could not imagine who on earth King Arthur intended to marry.

A FACE AT A TOURNAMENT

Sir Lancelot did not know that during one of his Welsh campaigns the king's heart had been won by the romantic beauty of Gwenevere, princess of Cameliard, and daughter of the rebel King Leodegrance. Arthur had been riding through one of the remote Welsh valleys on his way back to his camp, when his attention had been attracted by the sounds of lances clashing against armour. Riding towards the noise, Arthur found himself in the thick of a tournament, which was evidently being held to celebrate an extremely beautiful maiden, seated in the centre of a richly adorned pavilion. There was something about the girl's face which attracted the king from the first; he watched her with fascination and growing admiration as she awarded various prizes for gallantry and horseman-ship. At length Arthur was tempted to try his luck: he rode into the lists, and challenged one particularly cocksure knight, who had so far escaped defeat. The king took the precaution of pulling down his visor, so that he should not be recognized by Leodegrance's men; but his skill at arms was so remarkable, that the crowd soon began to murmur:

'This is a valiant knight indeed! There is no coat of arms upon his shield, and yet he fights as if he were at least a chieftain, if not a king.' One or two of the knights who had visited Arthur's court were struck by the brilliance of the unknown knight's horsemanship, and reminded of King Arthur of Camelot. But since Leodegrance and Arthur were known to be mortal enemies, it never occurred to them that Arthur himself could be present. So the king went undetected.

Gwenevere watched the tournament with growing

interest: in spite of her calm appearance, she was intrigued by the stranger, and asked several of her maids-of-honour who he was. But none of them could find out more than that he was evidently a foreigner, and by his speech, of gentle birth. When it was Arthur's turn to receive a prize, Gwenevere chided him gently on his closed visor.

'Surely a courteous knight would raise his visor to receive a prize from a lady's hands,' she said laughingly. Arthur hesitated, and decided to risk it; he lifted the iron visor and gazed proudly at the princess. Gwenevere hesitated.

'Surely this face is familiar?' she thought. At that moment a cry went up from the men-at-arms:

'Arthur Pendragon! Seize him!' Arthur had been recognized. A throng of angry knights surrounded him, and the situation was desperate. Drawing his sword, Arthur hacked and cut his way out of the mêlée, and leaping the barred gate at the end of the lists, set off at a gallop with half a dozen men of Cameliard in hot pursuit. Half to herself, Gwenevere murmured:

'God protect him!'

'Why, madam,' exclaimed her waiting-woman. 'He needs no protection! That is the famous Arthur, King of Camelot, who claims your father as one of his vassals. Surely you have heard of his insolent messages to your royal father demanding homage?'

'All the same,' whispered Gwenevere, 'I pray that he may escape, for he is alone in a hostile land, and the odds are against him.' Gwenevere's prayer was answered, and Arthur's fast horse outdistanced the warriors of Cameliard.

Despite the short moment for which he had seen her,

Gwenevere's face haunted Arthur. He listened eagerly to news from Wales, and lived in agonies in case she married one of the rebel chieftains. Lancelot's message suggested a cunning plan to him. He had heard that lately King Leodegrance had been hard pressed by the attacks of his rival, King Caradoc. Leodegrance was growing old, and could no longer lead his people into battle with the strength of his youth. Wales was full of rumours that Caradoc would defeat Leodegrance and annex his lands.

Arthur had never lost sight of his plan to make Leodegrance his vassal. Here was a chance to kill two birds with one stone! He would come to the help of Leodegrance against Caradoc, win his allegiance, and ask for the hand of the Princess Gwenevere. It all seemed very simple, sitting in his castle at Camelot. Arthur hoped that it would not be much more difficult to put the plan into practice.

ATTACK AT MIDNIGHT

But at the very frontiers of Wales, things started to go wrong. He learned that Caradoc had defeated Leodegrance in a pitched battle and had imprisoned the Princess Gwenevere in his own fastness high up in the mountains. People said he intended to marry her, and rule Cameliard himself.

'But Leodegrance?' demanded Arthur. 'Is the king dead?' Apparently Leodegrance was a prisoner in his own castle, guarded night and day by Caradoc's barbarians. Nobody thought he would survive very long in their hands. There was not a moment to lose, if Arthur's plan was to succeed. He forced his tired men to march on to the castle of Leodegrance in the heart of Cameliard. It was night when they discerned the dark shape of the castle battlements against the sky. Here and there a light glowed, where a sentry crouched over a fire.

'I want ten volunteers to scale those walls,' exclaimed Arthur. A dozen men immediately sprang forward, in spite of their fatigue. He chose the strongest, and told them to take off their mail, and leave behind all their weapons, except one dagger, which they were to carry between their teeth. The ten desperate men lined up before the king. Arthur himself had taken off his mail. So the king was going with them! Noiselessly the band crept to the side of the castle, and heaved each other up to the precarious footholds in the massive walls. Arthur led the way. He climbed like a cat, for he and Kay had become expert climbers in their childhood. He was actually at the top when one of the men missed his footing, and fell heavily to the ground. He stifled his groans, but the noise had alerted the sentries. Arthur sprang at the throat of the first man who appeared on the edge of the battlements, and toppled him over the parapet. Next over the wall, Bedevere seized the second sentry and threw him over the side. By the time the other sentries had appeared, all nine of the survivors were streaming across the roof of the castle, and separating on the staircases which led down into the heart of the stronghold. Bewildered in the darkness, baffled by these silent intruders, some of Caradoc's men could hardly believe that anyone *had* entered the castle by scaling the walls.

Angry disputes arose between those who had actually fought with the invaders, and felt their sharp daggers, and those who had arrived too late to believe that anything at all had happened. This gave Arthur the advantage he wanted. The nine men crept on into the depths of Leodegrance's imprisoned fortress, stabbing or strangling Caradoc's ruffians when they had to, but avoiding all unnecessary noise or bloodshed.

Arthur's army awaited silently ouside in the darkness. Suddenly a great barking among the camp dogs, and whinnying of the war-horses, warned them that something was happening behind them. At the very moment when the first cries and shouts reached them from within the castle, Arthur's army was attacked from behind! It was Caradoc in full force. The news of Arthur's quick march had been brought to him by one of his spies, and the cunning Welshman had immediately foreseen Arthur's plan.

'So Arthur Pendragon intends to rescue Leodegrance,' he thought. 'I will attack him in the rear at the moment when he assaults the castle.' Caradoc's plan would have succeeded to perfection if Arthur had been content with a straightforward attack on the stronghold. As it was, there were now two fierce battles, inside and outside the castle. Inside the castle Arthur had the advantage of surprise; outside it was Caradoc's men who had the advantage of their sudden and completely unexpected onslaught. The bitter conflict raged on the moonlit turf, and many of Arthur's brave men died at the hands of Caradoc's ruffians. Arthur's army was in fact outnumbered by the barbarians; but Arthur's knights considered themselves worth two of their enemies. They fought on against the heavy odds, and recovering from the first shock of the attack, turned the tables on Caradoc so well that he began to shout for assistance from the castle. But here his

soldiers were in no position to help him. One by one
Arthur seized the various strong-points in the fortress
until the castle itself was in his hands. In answer to
Caradoc's cries for assistance, the castle gates did indeed
open, and a gang of armed soldiers rushed out. But these
were not his own men – they were Arthur's knights, and
the soldiers of Leodegrance released from the dungeons!
Caradoc's fate was sealed. He found himself surrounded.
In despair he cried aloud that his gods had deserted him,
and transformed his own soldiers into the enemy. Super-
stitious like all pagans, Caradoc believed strongly in
omens; he felt that Arthur had magic on his side and that
there was no point in fighting him any longer. Sullenly,
Caradoc sheathed his sword, and gave the signal for
surrender.

'My gods deserted me in the hour of my need,' he said to
Arthur when he was brought before him in the great hall
of Leodegrance's castle. 'Henceforward I will worship your
God, for I see he has won you a great victory tonight.'
Thus Caradoc and all his vassals embraced Christianity,
and became subjects of Arthur. Arthur was flushed with
triumph at the success of his plan. As Caradoc knelt before
him and took the oath of allegiance, King Leodegrance
limped across the hall, leaning heavily on a stick. He had
been found chained to the wall in the darkest of the castle
dungeons, and Arthur could see that he had suffered
terribly from his imprisonment. The famous rebel king
looked like an old man. King Leodgrance knelt down
painfully before Arthur. His hands trembled as he placed
them between the king's.

'From the bottom of my heart I thank you for delivering
me from bondage, Arthur Pendragon. In gratitude for

this, I hereby become your vassal for the rest of my life. Never again will I seek to cast off the yoke of the Pendragons, for I see that they really are outstanding among the kings of Britain.' Arthur remembered the humiliations of his coronation, when the kings had repudiated him. What a contrast now, when two powerful kings had just taken the oath of allegiance of their own accord!

'As your liege lord, I would ask a favour of you, Leodegrance,' said Arthur. Leodegrance inclined his head. 'The hand of your daughter Gwenevere in marriage,' the king went on boldly. Leodegrance was delighted. It was an unexpected honour for a vanquished king to be allied to his conqueror in marriage. It was high time for Arthur to be returning to Camelot and the affairs of state which were piling up for him there. But without even considering the possibility that Gwenevere might refuse, Leodegrance agreed to send his daughter to the court, as soon as she had been fetched from the castle of Caradoc.

Confident that nothing could go wrong with his plans now, Arthur returned in triumph to Camelot.

But Gwenevere's feelings, when the news was brought to her, were not nearly so complacent. She felt extremely angry with her father for disposing of her so cold-bloodedly, for the sake of a firm alliance with the Pendragons. Gwenevere was young and romantic – she dreamt of a knight in armour rescuing her in distress and wooing her without knowing who she was. An arranged marriage between the daughter of the king of Cameliard and the king of Camelot seemed dull and distasteful. Gwenevere had almost forgotten what Arthur looked like.

She had only seen him for a moment at the tournament, and she persuaded herself that he would be ugly and unattractive. Altogether Gwenevere was in a disconsolate mood when she set out for Camelot in the richly adorned barge which was to bear her down the river. She supposed that Arthur would meet her himself somewhere on the way. But her ladies told her that she would meet Arthur for the first time at Camelot.

'I hope it will not be too much trouble for the great king to walk up the aisle on his wedding-day,' she said crossly, flouncing away and withdrawing herself to the opposite end of the barge. Gazing over the side, it was Gwenevere who first noticed the four armed horsemen riding along the bank. Their lances glinted in the sun. She saw that their visors were down – a curious sight in a peaceful country, where knights did not generally ride four abreast in battle array. Gwenevere felt slightly frightened. She turned to go back to her women. At that moment an arrow whistled through the air and landed in the wooden deck of the barge. It quivered beside her and the princess gazed in horror at the menacing sight. It was an ambush! And they had only one armed guard on board. The soldier did his best against the four knights, but he could not hold his own against so many. He fell to the ground groaning, while the leading knight mounted the barge and dragged Gwenevere to the bank. She screamed for help.

'There is no one to hear your cries, my lady,' said the man grimly. 'Meanwhile those pretty jewels will make a fine booty.'

'Not so fast!' said a stern voice behind him. Starting round, Gwenevere saw another knight in black armour, mounted on a magnificent black horse, with his lance

43

poised in his hand. The four robber knights were inclined to dismiss this lone attacker with contempt. What could he do against so many? But when they felt the strength of his blows, they changed their tune. This was a devil in armour, not an ordinary knight. Two knights he pierced to the heart, the third fell mortally wounded, and the fourth surrendered at his feet. Gwenevere found herself freed from the bonds which the robbers had roped round her, and set on her feet. Her rescuer put up his visor with a weary gesture, and wiped the sweat from his forehead.

Gwenevere found herself looking at the most hand-some face in Britain – Sir Lancelot himself.

'Oh, this is the romance of which I dreamt,' she thought to herself. 'In any case I cannot let this knight disappear without some word of thanks,' she added, to excuse herself. Gwenevere invited Lancelot to come aboard her barge and have his wounds, such as they were, and they were few, tended by her women.

'I would rather have them tended by your own hands,' replied Sir Lancelot ardently. He was dazzled by Gwenevere's beauty, which far exceeded any other woman he had ever seen. He looked down at her small white hands. Then he turned pale. Winking up at him was the magnificent royal ruby, which Arthur had given to Leodegrance to place upon Gwenevere's finger as a token of his love. Lancelot's first instinct was to throw himself on his knees before his future queen. But some fatal impulse for adventure prevented him. He, too, like Gwenevere, yearned for romance; and what could be more romantic than the secret love of a knight for his future queen? Little knowing that Gwenevere had fallen head-over-heels in love with him, Lancelot agreed to ride with the princess in the barge.

How quickly the journey to Camelot passed for both of them! Gwenevere dared not think of her marriage, or of Arthur. She tried to blot out the future by concentrating on the happiness of the present with her unknown lover. It was a bitter moment for Gwenevere when they reached Camelot and Lancelot revealed himself to her as the famous knight of Arthur's court, famous as far as Cameliard for his success with the ladies. Where were her dreams of romance now? Her romantic rescuer had probably delivered princesses by the dozen in his time, and made the same ardent speeches to them. In her unhappiness and disillusion, Gwenevere said as much to Lancelot. But Lancelot's adventure had recoiled upon him. For the first time he too felt the pangs of real love.

'Oh, you have reason to reproach me, Gwenevere,' he said passionately. 'For I should never have come near you. I should have rescued you and ridden off. For who could see you every day for a week and not fall in love with you? What was meant to be a lighthearted adventure has turned into a tragic love, for me as well as you. Yet I cannot steal you from Arthur, for he is my liege lord, and I have sworn an oath to him.'

Gwenevere saw from his tortured face that he spoke the truth. In spite of her breaking heart, she smiled bravely and said that if he was strong enough to perform his duty to his king, she had enough courage to be loyal to her affianced husband. So Gwenevere stepped calmly from the barge at Camelot and accepted the cheers of the crowd with perfect dignity and grace. The people who acclaimed the bride of Arthur little knew that Gwenevere and Lancelot were doomed to love each other in secret for the rest of their lives.

The Marriage of Gwenevere and Arthur

Nowadays it seems cruel that Gwenevere should have been compelled to marry Arthur instead of Lancelot, whom she loved. But one must remember that Gwenevere had been brought up to respect her father and his wishes. As a princess, she was conscious that more depended on her marriage than depended on the marriage of an ordinary girl; for royal marriages were used to make alliances and join two kingdoms together. By marrying Arthur, Gwenevere would unite Camelot and Cameliard; if she broke her betrothal, Arthur and Leodegrance would be permanently estranged, and there might even be a war between them, to avenge the insult to Arthur's honour. Gwenevere was too honourable to bring this fate upon her father, and so she determined to keep her love for Lancelot hidden deep in her heart.

In his turn Lancelot understood the importance of his knightly vow to the king, and he knew the dreadful consequences which would follow if he broke it. He would have incurred the wrath of God upon him, and he would have been outcast from Arthur's kingdom for ever by the rules of chivalry. Instead, Lancelot swore to serve Gwenevere all his life. Lancelot was doing what many another knight unsuccessful in love had done before him – pledging himself to the lifelong service of his beloved.

The marriage of Arthur and Gwenevere was celebrated with great ceremony in the cathedral by the archbishop. The beauty of the queen called forth universal admiration from Arthur's knights, who felt that she would bring all the grace and dignity to the court which had previously been lacking. No hint of Gwenevere's secret sorrow appeared on her lovely face, as she walked down the aisle of the cathedral on the arm of the king; she was careful to avoid Lancelot's steady gaze, as she passed between the ranks of the king's knights.

'Long live our gracious Queen Gwenevere!' Lancelot was the first to raise the loyal cry on the king's wedding day.

KING LEODEGRANCE'S STRANGE WEDDING PRESENT

'That is the strangest sight in the world!' exclaimed Arthur to Merlin. They were sitting in a deep embrasure in the castle walls, gazing at the road which wound up to the castle from the town. Four ox carts were struggling along the road, weighed down by an enormous burden.

'A Round Table,' continued the king. 'Yes, it's a huge Round Table.'

Merlin sprang up from his chair and stared out of the window in great excitement. 'It must be the famous Round Table of King Leodegrance!' he said. 'This famous table was specially made to the king's requirements to hold two hundred and fifty knights, the flower of Welsh knighthood. I never thought to see the day when Leodegrance parted with the Round Table.' But after a great deal of reflection, the King of Cameliard had decided to send the Round Table to Camelot, as a token of his loyalty to Arthur, and as a wedding present for his daughter. The days in which Leodegrance could summon up two hundred and fifty knights were long since past; the effects of numerous wars with pagans and chieftains had been to reduce his chivalry to nearer fifty than two hundred and fifty. The empty seats at the table mocked him. He decided to pass the table on to a younger man.

Arthur received the gift with joy.

'This table is an inspiration to me,' he told Gwenevere and Merlin. 'You know that it is my dearest wish to drive the invaders back into the sea, and extend my kingdom from shore to shore. I shall found the Fellowship of the Round Table. Every knight who takes the oath of the Round Table shall be pledged to dedicate his life to the service of God, the hammering of his enemies and the protection of the weak.'

Merlin nodded in agreement.

'The Round Table should stand for all that is best in chivalry,' he answered. 'In the days of Leodegrance's prime it stood for high adventure. There are still many adventures to be had in Britain today, and many battles to be fought before the pagans are routed and the evil witches cast down.'

Between them Arthur and Merlin planned a triple oath for the Knights of the Round Table.

First to step forward to swear the oath of the Round Table was Sir Lancelot. As he did so a clap of thunder resounded through the castle hall, and the room was plunged in darkness. When the gloom cleared it could be seen that above each seat of the Round Table a name was written in letters of gold. Many of the names were still unknown to Arthur. Merlin solved the mystery.

'This miracle shows that God's blessing is upon the Round Table,' explained the wizard. 'It will be many years before every place is filled at the table, for as yet your knighthood does not number anything like two hundred and fifty. But in time every place shall be filled.' Then Merlin pointed to one seat, above which no name was written. As he pointed, letters of fire formed over the seat:

'No one shall sit here, unless he be the best knight in all the world.'

'What can this mean?' exclaimed the king, crossing himself.

'That is the Seat Perilous,' said the wizard. 'Even Sir Lancelot may not sit in that seat.' For the time being he refused to say more.

Then all the king's knights took their appointed places, and swore the triple oath of the Round Table. Following Sir Lancelot, there was Sir Kay and Sir Bedevere, Sir Gawaine, Arthur's proud nephew, Sir Egremont, Sir Walter, and many others. Last of all came the young Mordred, the child of the usurper and Morgan Le Fay, who had been abandoned by his mother when she escaped from the court. Merlin had tried to persuade Arthur to banish the boy Mordred, saying that he came of evil stock. But Arthur had been confident that he could bring up Mordred to forget his evil parentage. He had ignored Merlin's prophecies, and lavished as much kindness on Mordred as if he had been his own son.

However, Mordred was a sullen, unresponsive boy. He accepted Arthur's kindness as if it was his due, and meanwhile brooded in secret on the fancied slights and wrongs which had been dealt him. In particular, Mordred was jealous of Sir Lancelot for his popularity. Many a time Mordred vowed to get even with Sir Lancelot, if it took him a lifetime. But Arthur was blind to Mordred's faults; he continued to favour him, and trust him with important missions, in spite of all Merlin's predictions.

The shape of the Round Table had been carefully designed by Leodegrance, in the days of his power, to give every knight equal precedence. As the table was round, no one knight could claim to be sitting higher up than any other. Already at Arthur's court petty jealousies and squabbles were breaking out: but the Round Table solved these rivalries for the time being.

'Thanks to Leodegrance,' thought the king, 'I shall at least have peace at my court, however hard the heathens press the kingdom.'

The founding of the Round Table was the beginning of a great age of adventure such as never before had been seen in Britain. Each knight had sworn to serve God, honour the king and protect the weak, and every year at Pentecost all the knights together renewed their oath. Then the king would ask what great adventures had been had during the past year. Wonderful tales were related which enthralled the court, and made them marvel at the great courage of the Knights of the Round Table.

5

SIR LANCELOT AND
THE MAID OF ASTOLAT

*K*ing Arthur banged his fist on the Round Table.

'I can no longer endure this plague-spot on the map of my kingdom!' he cried. 'Who will go out and govern the Waste Land for me? Year by year reports of the Waste Land grow more gloomy. No crops grow there. Houses fall down in rack and ruin. Yet these reports are always brought to me by pilgrims and travellers. The inhabitants never complain. I would have expected daily pleas for help from the people. But in four years I have not had a word since the death of the Lord of Astolat.'

Sir Lancelot stood up.

'Let me go to the Waste Land, my liege,' he cried. 'I yearn for an adventure to test my courage. Send me out as your governor.' Little as Arthur liked parting with his chief knight and closest friend, Sir Lancelot was the ideal man for the task, brave, enterprising and just. Sir Lancelot knelt before Gwenevere and dedicated the adventure to her. Then, disdaining to take a large force of soldiers with him, he set out at once for the Waste Land.

Here he was struck by the desolation of the land. The very blades of grass were yellow and withered. The trees looked as if they had one and all been struck by lightning.

There was scarcely a green leaf to be seen. The animals, from dogs to horses, from hens to sheep, were thin and mangy. As for houses, they were indeed going to rack and ruin. The whole place looked as if it had a curse upon it. As Sir Lancelot rode through the silent villages, only the chink of his armour told him that he was not dreaming the whole situation. Sir Lancelot's horse was weary, and in need of food and water, so he stopped at a tavern, determined to question the innkeeper closely about the state of the land. To his surprise, the front door was bolted securely.

'They cannot expect much custom here,' thought Sir Lancelot. Then he noticed a man peering out at him from an upper window.

'Come down, sirrah, and attend to my horse,' he called angrily. 'I have ridden a long way, and I do not intend to ride any farther.' In answer, the man scowled at him, but said nothing. Nothing Sir Lancelot said could draw any kind of response from him and he was forced to ride on. But in every village, not a single human being would address a word to him. As night fell, he laid himself down under a mouldering hay-rick, and fell asleep.

He was woken a few hours later by the feeling that somebody was watching him. Half asleep still, Sir Lancelot reached for his sword, and looked round. A young girl, pale and melancholy, but still of great beauty, was gazing at him mournfully. Her large and lovely eyes were filled with tears, but like all the other inhabitants of this strange land, she spoke not a word.

'By all the saints!' exclaimed Sir Lancelot. 'This is the weirdest adventure which ever a man had. Is this whole country dumb?' The maiden sighed, but still said nothing. Sir Lancelot seized the girl and cried fiercely:

'Speak to me, girl, else I shall not hesitate to force words from you with my sword.' The girl began to weep bitterly.

'Alas, alas, Sir Knight,' she moaned, 'you have compelled me to break silence, and for this I shall be killed this very night. And yet from the first moment I set eyes on you sleeping, my heart was filled with such love for you, that I felt it was worth risking death to remain near to you.' Sir Lancelot disregarded her loving words, which he thought might be a trap.

'What death is threatening you?' he asked in a softer tone. 'Perhaps I can deliver you, and this whole miserable country.' The maiden quieted her sobs and leant her fair head on Sir Lancelot's shoulder. She told him that her name was Elaine, and that she was called the Maid of Astolat. Sir Lancelot was a mile outside the town of Astolat, of which her father had been the lord of the manor. Since his death, great sorrow had come to Astolat and the surrounding countryside: for a Black Knight, of fearful aspect, had ravaged the villages, terrorizing the innocent people, and demanding money and food from them. This Black Knight had proved a worse master even than the dreaded Saxons themselves; he seemed to have some magic power by which he defeated all the knights who were bold enough to challenge him. So powerful was he, that no one dared disobey his commands, and when he commanded his unwilling subjects to take a vow of silence, no one dared break it. He had put a curse upon the country, by which no living creature could flourish.

'You see,' said Elaine tearfully, 'he has us in his power for ever. We dare not speak and explain our peril, for he will surely kill us. Already he has slain fourteen brave knights who fought with him up there by the Chapel

Dolorous.' She pointed to a ruined chapel on the edge of a forest a mile or so away.

Adventure, however dangerous, was always welcome to Lancelot; he felt his blood boil at this story of oppression. Without delay he told the maiden to lead him to the knight's lair.

'Alas, alas,' wept Elaine. 'Do not fight him, fair knight, for he is invincible. Fly while there is still time.'

'I must keep the oath of the Round Table,' replied Sir Lancelot proudly. Seeing that Sir Lancelot would not be warned, Elaine explained to him that he would have to kneel in the Chapel Dolorous all night in prayer, surrounded by the shields of the Black Knight's victims. At dawn he would hear the thunder of a horse's hoofs, and the Black Knight would gallop forth from the forest, eager to overthrow yet another challenger. Elaine confessed that she had watched the Black Knight defeat four strong knights in one morning. Then she began to weep again, weeping for Sir Lancelot and for her people.

Sir Lancelot brushed her tears away gently, and made his way to the Chapel Dolorous. The chapel lay in a lonely place, with the forest on one side and the cliff face, falling sheer away, on the other. It was about two o'clock in the morning when Sir Lancelot picked his way into the chancel. In the cold moonlight, he noticed many shields hanging on the broken walls; and one or two crests he thought he recognized. He breathed a quick prayer for the repose of the souls of the knights who had met their death in this ungodly place. Then he saw skulls and bones littering the pavement, and even Sir Lancelot felt a pang of fear.

Four hours till dawn. The knight knelt in prayer before

54

the high altar, listening for any sound which would herald the approach of his enemy. As the first rays of sun struck the eastern window of the chapel, he heard the sound of a horse's hoofs, as Elaine had prophesied. Quickly Sir Lancelot girded himself in his armour, and strode boldly outside to meet his fate.

The sight which met Sir Lancelot's eyes would have struck terror into any other heart: the Black Knight was mounted on a huge black horse, and he towered over Sir Lancelot's head. However, Sir Lancelot did not flinch from the charge, but stood his ground, and dealt a mighty blow at the Black Knight's shield. He succeeded in denting it to such good effect that the Black Knight had to cast it away. Try as he might, he could not reach Sir Lancelot from his horse; so he leaped from the saddle and engaged in a ferocious hand-to-hand fight on the ground. While Elaine held her breath, Sir Lancelot slowly beat the Black Knight back to the chapel, and with a final swing of his sword, pierced his visor. The Black Knight fell to the ground, and his helmet rolled off. To Sir Lancelot's joy, the thrust of his sword had pierced the Black Knight's throat and, with a last groan, the oppressor closed his eyes and died.

Elaine rushed out of her hiding-place, weeping with relief, and flung her arms round Sir Lancelot's neck.

'Saviour!' she cried. 'You have saved Astolat! All this country is yours now, you are the new lord of the manor.'

'This is my country already,' replied Sir Lancelot between gritted teeth, disengaging her arms from his neck. 'King Arthur of Camelot sent me to be governor here for six months, to restore the land to prosperity.' He had become so pale that Elaine was alarmed. As she anxiously examined the rents in his armour, the knight groaned aloud, and sank to the ground in a faint. To Elaine's horror, she found that the whole of one side of his leg had been laid open by the Black Knight's sword.

She ordered five serving-men to bear Sir Lancelot to her tower at Astolat, and lay him on her couch.

'This is the new lord of Astolat,' she told the people. 'He has rid this land of the peril of the Black Knight in a fierce fight at the Chapel Dolorous. He has been wounded, and it is my duty to nurse him back to health.' Elaine was secretly determined to wed Sir Lancelot. Beneath her innocent face and sad expression lay a strong will and a selfish nature. When she saw that all her ministrations did not make Sir Lancelot's heart soften towards her, she decided to invoke the help of magic.

While the knight slumbered, Elaine poured a love potion into his medicine. She smiled to see him drain it to the dregs, and waited for the potion to take effect. Sure enough, Sir Lancelot immediately seized her hand and told her that she was the most beautiful girl he had ever seen.

'More beautiful than Queen Gwenevere?' asked Elaine coyly, for Sir Lancelot had sung the praises of his queen to her so often that she was extremely jealous of Gwenevere. Sir Lancelot hesitated. There had been a time when no woman in the world surpassed the queen in his eyes; but now he felt a new love burning within him for Elaine.

'You are fairest of them all, Elaine,' replied Sir Lancelot ardently. 'I would that I could win you for my bride.'

'You know full well that I have never loved any other knight since I first set my eyes on you, my lord,' answered Elaine quickly. 'Our marriage would please the people of

Astolat as much as it would please me. No one has ever been as popular as you here, Lancelot.' All thought of Gwenevere had vanished from Sir Lancelot's mind. He pressed a kiss on Elaine's white hand, and agreed to marry her as soon as possible.

As Elaine had prophesied, the news was received with great rejoicing in Astolat, and the church bells, silent for so long, rang out to celebrate the betrothal. Elaine walked proudly through the town on the arm of her new husband, satisfied that her scheme to trap Sir Lancelot had worked.

The magic potion made Lancelot a devoted husband. The crops of the Waste Land grew again, the animals grew fat and the trees and grass returned to their old greenness. All this time Lancelot spared not a thought for Camelot and Arthur. He remembered Gwenevere only as a beautiful woman whom he had courted long ago, but no recollection of their love disturbed the peace of his life with Elaine. Elaine smiled complacently to see her success.

Nevertheless, whenever Lancelot rode abroad on business, she felt a small pang of apprehension. She irritated him by persistent questions and incessant possessiveness. Elaine had a reason for wanting to keep Lancelot at her side, for she was expecting a child in the spring, and she hoped to chain Lancelot to her for ever by fatherhood. In the meantime she guarded her secret.

'Camelot and the queen shall never claim him if I can help it,' she swore to herself.

But the strands which bound the destinies of Lancelot and Gwenevere together were too strong even for her magic potion. Lancelot was actually riding in the forest of Astolat, near the Chapel Dolorous, when he awakened from his enchantment.

'Take that! And that!' he heard someone shout. The voice was familiar and it stirred strange memories. He spurred his horse and galloped into the clearing. He found Sir Gawaine and Sir Bedevere, defending themselves valiantly against a gang of robbers who had ambushed them. The two were hard pressed, but with Sir Lancelot to assist them, they put the gang to flight. All this time, Sir Lancelot was unrecognizable. But as soon as he lifted his helmet, Sir Bedevere and Sir Gawaine greeted him with delight.

'Our comrade!' they cried. 'It has been two long years since we saw you.'

'Two years,' he repeated. 'Is it really so long since I was at Camelot? In that case, I shall return with you this very night.' In a flash, Lancelot's love for Elaine seemed to have vanished. Memories of Gwenevere, his true love, came flooding back.

Meanwhile, Elaine, at her spinning-wheel, shivered as if a ghost were walking over her grave. She felt a presentiment of evil, and at once sent out a squire to look for the Lord Lancelot. He came back with the news that Lord Lancelot had been seen riding north at a gallop, with two other noble knights in armour. Elaine screamed. The knights must have come to summon back her husband. Elaine fell in a swoon to the floor, and for many weeks lay between life and death.

All this was unknown to Lancelot, his heart filled with joy at the prospect of seeing Gwenevere again. Lancelot's reunion with Arthur was a precious moment. Sir Lancelot dropped on one knee before him and renewed the great oath of the Round Table to him. He explained his long absence with references to magic spells and difficulties

58

with the Saxons; and he told Arthur that order had been restored once more in the Waste Land. Arthur thought it wiser to ask no further questions.

But several months later a mournful sight greeted the eyes of those who watched the river. A barge, filled with flowers, was seen floating down towards Camelot. Along the bank walked weeping women, who raised their lamentations to heaven, and filled the air with their cries.

The queen's anger was terrible when she learned that the barge contained no other than Sir Lancelot's wife, who had pined away for him, and finally died on the journey to Camelot.

At length she set out to pay her respects to the funeral procession of Sir Lancelot's wife. The pale face of Elaine, laid out in the barge amid flowers and wreaths, moved her in spite of herself. She laid a bunch of violets on the bier, and murmured a prayer for the repose of Elaine's soul.

That night at dinner, everyone noticed the coldness which Gwenevere showed to Lancelot. At the end of dinner, Gwenevere turned to Arthur and said in a loud, clear voice:

'My lord, what punishment would you give a knight who deserted his wife?'

'A knight who deserts his wife is guilty of breaking the oath of the Round Table,' replied Arthur sternly. 'That knight would be drummed out of my court.'

'Behold the knight of whom I speak,' said Gwenevere coldly, pointing at Lancelot, who shrank back.

'Is this true?' demanded the king. Sir Lancelot was too amazed and ashamed to speak. How deeply he regretted the selfish impulse which had led him to desert Elaine. As he sat there, silent, with his head hung low, a solemn procession wound its way into the hall, bearing the body of Elaine. Even in death Elaine looked beautiful, and many were the angry looks which were directed to Sir Lancelot. Arthur's face reflected the extent of his disappointment in him.

At the very moment when he had decided to strip Sir Lancelot of his spurs, the worst punishment of all, an aged woman forced her way to the king and unfolded her remarkable story. She said that the Maid of Astolat had bought a love potion from her to win the hand of a noble knight in marriage. The maid had admitted that that magic alone would win the affections of this knight, who had already told her that he was dedicated to the service of his queen. Several months later she had watched the maid leave the church of Astolat triumphantly with her bridegroom and had recognized Sir Lancelot.

The king's face cleared, and Gwenevere's relief was obvious. She begged Lancelot to forgive her for her cruelty.

Lancelot replied despondently that he could forgive her, but not himself. Merlin had often hinted to Lancelot that his self-indulgence would ruin him. In despair at the blot on his honour, Lancelot vowed himself to a life of penance until he had atoned for the death of Elaine.

6

THE WAGER OF BALIN AND BORS

*T*he twin sons of the King of Brittany stood on the shore of France and gazed at the two ships which stood at anchor, ready to take them away from their native land: the one to Ireland and the court of King Brian, the other to Britain and the court of the Round Table. Bors shook Balin by the hand.

'It will not be long before we have won our spurs,' he said; 'then we shall meet again and have many splendid adventures together. I swear it.'

'I wager I will be the better fighter when we next meet,' said Balin. The King of Brittany was lately dead, and the brothers had decided to leave the country to seek their fortune abroad. Their elder brother, Tristram, had already departed for the court of King Mark of Cornwall. But such a close bond united Bors and Balin that they had put off their departure until the last possible moment. Even when the ships had weighed anchor, the brothers still waved at each other and shouted encouraging messages across the ever-widening sea.

'God-speed to Ireland,' Balin's voice came to Bors faintly. 'God-speed to Britain, Brother,' he shouted back. Soon the white sails of the Irish ship had disappeared over the horizon.

Alas for the high hopes of the brothers. Bors found the Irish court a hard test for his powers of endurance. His Breton accent was considered ridiculous, and they teased him for his old-fashioned ways. Balin was undergoing the same torments at Camelot. Balin, the elder brother by half an hour, had always been the leader. If Bors had known that Balin was enduring the same treatment without complaining, his own resolution might have grown. As it was, his spirit broke and he decided to run away.

Late at night, when his squire's duties were finished, he stole out from the chamber where the squires slept and took a horse from the royal stables. He rode hard for the coast, where he intended to stow away in the first ship which would take him to Brittany. But when he came to the coast a strange sight met his eyes. Huge bonfires were alight on the seashore and wild men in horned helmets with flowing golden hair were feasting in the firelight. From the many tales which he had heard, Bors had no difficulty in recognizing these men as the dreaded Norsemen themselves. Their speech was rough and unintelligible, but their actions spoke for themselves: they had evidently sacked the coast villages, and were about to set sail in their long ships with their booty and prisoners.

A daring plan occurred to Bors. With his yellow hair and blue eyes, he might easily have been taken for a Norseman, and indeed the Irish had sometimes called him the Viking as a joke. While the Norsemen infested the Irish Sea, no other boats would dare put out to sea – and so it was a question of stowing away in the long ships or not at all. Bors did not hesitate. He strode calmly forward on to the seashore and took his place on the outside of a small group of Norsemen who were roistering and drinking round a bonfire. Bors did not think there was much danger of his being discovered as long as they were drunk.

An hour later there was a general move towards the boats, and Bors was able to mix quietly with the crowd. He seated himself inconspicuously in the prow. One or two stared at him curiously, but whenever a question was addressed to him, he pretended to be talking to someone at his elbow, and ignored it. In this way Bors managed to pass a week at sea, travelling he knew not where. He hoped passionately that the Vikings would decide to raid the coast of Brittany.

On his eighth day at sea, however, his attention was attracted by one of the prisoners, who was lying bound hand and foot in the bottom of the boat. This was an extremely beautiful girl, who, by her rich clothes and jewellery, must have been the daughter of one of the Irish chieftains. Bors was greatly struck by her remarkable loveliness, and he wished there was some way of rescuing her from her bondage. Later that night, when most of the Vikings were sleeping, he crept down into the bottom of the boat, and whispered to the girl:

'Are you awake?' The girl started at the sound of his voice, for, unlike the Norsemen, he spoke in Gaelic.

'You are not a Viking,' she whispered. 'I can tell by your speech. Who are you, and where do you come from?'

'Shsh, lest they hear us. I am a fugitive from the court of King Brian. My father, the King of Brittany, sent me there to learn the arts of chivalry. Alas, I was faint-hearted and homesick, and I ran away. When I saw the long ships, I decided to disguise myself as a Viking and stow away.'

'You are not faint-hearted,' replied the girl, gazing at Bors with admiration. 'If you had another chance, I know that you would win your spurs. I am Deirdre, princess of Ireland, and daughter of King Brian. You passed by me once at the court, your eyes filled with tears at the rough words of my father's men: and I was filled with sympathy for you in your loneliness.'

Bors kissed the princess's hand in the darkness. He swore to rescue her from the clutches of the Vikings.

A week later, in the small hours of the morning, the Viking ships stole into a lonely creek. They were clearly expected, for piles of captured armour lay on the shore, and horses were tethered in dozens on the beach. Bors guessed their plan: the Vikings were going to disguise themselves as knights and so roam the country undetected until the time came to strike. He marvelled at their cunning, and wondered what treacherous ally had placed the armour on the shore. However, if armour could disguise a Norseman, it could also disguise a Breton! With the rest of the Vikings, Bors arrayed himself in a breastplate and a helmet, and chose a horse. Then he had an inspiration: seeing that no one was guarding the prisoners very closely, he crept round to Deirdre and cut her bonds with his knife. The guard shouted at him in Norse, but Bors shook his head imperiously, as though he was only carrying out orders. Then he led Deirdre to the pile of armour, and arrayed her in the smallest suit of armour he could find. The disguise was perfect! Deirdre suffered the discomfort in silence, upheld by her love for Bors.

The Vikings had landed where Bristol is today, and the column of knights was heading across the most fertile land

in Arthur's kingdom. They intended to sack the castle of
Bristol itself, in revenge for a defeat which Arthur had
inflicted on them two years before. The news of their
landing reached Arthur at Camelot. Arthur immediately
ordered his army into the field.

Balin watched the preparations with envy. He resolved
to steal a horse and armour and follow the king into battle.
When Arthur set forth, the last knight to join his ranks was
no other than Balin.

But search as Arthur might, he could not find the
Norsemen. Arthur was on the point of turning back, when
it occurred to him to send a couple of knights out as spies.
He signed to Balin and two others. This was Balin's
chance: if only he could find some trace of the Viking
force, he would have proved himself a worthy knight and
would be judged fit to receive his spurs. He left his two
companions, and struck out for himself across country.

Fortune favoured Balin. Watering his horse at a lonely
inn one night, he overheard two pantry boys discussing
the Vikings.

'I know one thing, Godric,' said the first in an
undertone. 'The king will never find the Vikings while he
continues to look for savages in winged helmets. Our
master has seen to that.'

'True enough,' replied his companion with a cynical
laugh. 'All those suits of armour have gone from the loft, I
see. Our master is a traitor to the king, but we are well
paid to keep our mouths shut about it, so I will not be the
first to spread the news.' Balin resolved to ride back to the
king as fast as possible, and disclose his sensational news.

He was about a mile from the royal camp when he fell in
with two knights, clad in armour from top to toe. They

were riding slowly along the highway, as if the route was unfamiliar to them, and Balin, glad to have company, asked if he might ride along beside them. To his surprise neither knight answered. Their visors were down, so that it was impossible to tell their expressions, but Balin felt a sudden wild suspicion! Could these knights be two Vikings in disguise?

His suspicions were confirmed when the taller knight of the two said something to his companion in a foreign tongue. Although they were two to one, Balin reined in his horse and challenged them to speak or defend themselves. The smaller knight shrank back in fear, but his companion immediately aimed a mighty blow at Balin's shield. The fight was on! Balin was convinced that he had detected two Viking spies, and not knowing that Arthur's army was even now on the march towards him, he defended himself as if the whole safety of England depended upon it. The battle was violent and long – back and forwards went the blows, without either side seeming to gain any advantage. All this time the smaller knight took no part in the combat, but watched in terror from the roadside. At last Balin managed to pierce the breastplate of his enemy, and plunge his lance into his opponent's breast. Although he himself was bleeding in several places, he still had enough strength to follow up the blow with another, and another and another, pressing home his advantage until the Viking fell from his horse. As the army of Arthur rounded the corner, Balin leaped from his charger, and placed his foot on the fallen knight.

'What fight is this?' exclaimed the king. Balin told him what he had heard, and how he had found two strange knights talking in a foreign tongue, who had refused to explain their presence, but had immediately attacked him when he challenged them. All this time Balin's visor was down, so that the king was under the impression he was talking to one of the Knights of the Round Table. But when Arthur congratulated him, Balin flung up his helmet and revealed himself. The king was amazed to see the Breton squire who had been so despised at court. He congratulated Balin on his courage, and knighted him at once. At that moment a deep groan attracted their attention to the fallen knight. Balin went down and wrenched off his helmet. A terrible sight met his eyes: the fallen knight was no other than Bors his brother!

Balin's grief was pitiful to see! 'Oh, Bors,' he groaned. 'I have won my wager. I was indeed the better fighter. But I would to God I had never learned to bear arms: so I might have avoided killing my own brother.' In vain he tried to staunch his brother's wounds: Bors's life was ebbing away fast, and he only just had enough strength to explain his strange story. He just had time to warn Balin against the Vikings, when his voice failed, and he sank back lifeless into his brother's arms. Then a loud cry from the bank directed Balin's attention to the other knight. To his amazement the knight half hobbled, half ran towards the corpse of Bors and cast himself upon the body, weeping and wailing, as if his heart was broken. Deirdre, for it was she, cast off her helmet, and showed her tear-stained face to Balin.

'Murderer!' she cried. 'You have murdered your brother. Many times he has told me about you – Balin, his favourite brother. Little did I think that his brother would repay his devotion by killing him. Bors was no Viking. We were escaping together from their clutches – and now you have killed him.' In vain Balin begged Deirdre's forgiveness, she would not be comforted. Arthur took Deirdre gently by the arm, and heard her story and promised to give her clothing which suited her high rank, and find a ship to take her back to her native land. Then he lifted her up on to his own horse, and directed one of his squires to lead her back to Queen Gwenevere at Camelot. Balin gazed after her with anguish – for in that short moment her beauty had won his heart, as it had won the heart of his brother. He knew that she would never listen to his words of love while she believed him to be a murderer.

Deeply depressed, Balin followed Arthur and the rest of the knights who set off to attack the Vikings. The kindly Sir Bedevere tried to comfort him, by assuring him that it was impossible to recognize anyone in a suit of armour; but Balin could not forgive himself for his brother's death. In the fight with the Norsemen, Balin distinguished himself for his reckless bravery and took so many risks with his life that it looked as though he wanted to be killed. His courage turned the tide of the battle, and the marauders were driven back to their long ships in full flight. But still Balin was haunted by the thought of Bors's death, and all Arthur's words of comfort were in vain.

However, when the victorious army reached Camelot, the first to congratulate Balin on his courage was the Princess Deirdre herself. Gwenevere, with her kindness and common sense, had made the princess realize that Balin was innocent of his brother's death. Deirdre curtsied low to the knight, and begged his pardon so humbly that tears came into his eyes. Three weeks later a boat was leaving for Ireland, but Deirdre had found Balin's company so enjoyable that she was loath to leave

Camelot. She decided to spend the rest of her life in Britain, as the wife of Sir Balin.

7

SIR GAWAINE AND
THE GREEN KNIGHT

Jealousy was to be the undoing of the Round Table.
Fortunately its end was as yet far off. But already the
pangs of envy gnawed at two of the chief knights of the
court. Mordred was consumed by jealousy of Lancelot,
and secretly coveted the throne for himself. He made
himself believe that Arthur had stolen the crown from his
father, and that he should rightly be king. Mordred
managed to infect another knight with his pernicious
envy. Gawaine, the king's nephew, was a noble fighter
and a loyal friend; but he was proud and quick to take
offence, always ready to draw his sword if he thought he
was being insulted. Mordred suggested to Gawaine that
Arthur singled out Lancelot when he should have
favoured Gawaine. He repeated things which Arthur was
supposed to have said to the rest of the knights about
Gawaine.

'I would have given the command of the eastern
marches to Gawaine, but of course Lancelot is so much
the better general that I had no choice.' Gawaine brooded
on this. It was intolerable that he should be slighted! He
listened avidly to all the gossip which Mordred repeated.
He refused even to eat at the Round Table in the evenings,

70

but retired into his chamber and sulked. Arthur soon noticed Gawaine's absence. He sent a peremptory message ordering him to take his seat at the banquet. Gawaine stalked into the hall, with his lower lip stuck out. He looked the picture of obstinacy. He made no obeisance to Gwenevere, and did not even bow to the king. Gawaine flounced over to his seat and threw himself down. He did not deign to touch his food, but waved it away rudely, saying that it was ill-cooked and ill-served.

It was the Feast of Pentecost. The royal kitchens had taken especial pains to make the banquet worthy of the occasion. Even the pantry boys started to cast black looks at Gawaine for his rudeness. Arthur certainly was not going to tolerate this sort of behaviour. Pentecost was the traditional time for the commencement of an adventure. Petitioners had flocked to Camelot with their tales of distress. Arthur decided that a rousing adventure would take Gawaine out of himself. But every time Arthur appealed to Gawaine to take on some task, the knight refused him roughly. At last the king's patience failed.

'You have a strange way of honouring your oath!' he said sharply. 'I thought you had sworn to dedicate yourself to adventure in the service of others. Six times I have called upon you, and six times you have shaken me off. Leave the court, Gawaine, and do not return until you have got rid of this black mood.' The knight flushed at the rebuke. Without a word he left the Round Table and strode forth angrily into the night, resolved to have his revenge on Arthur and all the rest of the knights. Jealousy of Lancelot, inflamed by Mordred's mischief-making, had made Gawaine quite unreasonable. He rode northwards at a hot pace, without having any clear idea of where he was going. At the end of a week his anger had abated, and he felt ashamed of himself for his ungracious behaviour to his sovereign. He decided to seek an adventure on his own, and prove that he was worthy of the Round Table.

Not long after this Gawaine found himself in the famous forest of Broceliande, one of the wildest parts of the north of Britain. Somewhere within the forest was reputed to lie a famous fountain, whose waters were so sweet and healing that they could cure any illness. Gawaine thought it would be a noble deed to find this fountain, and bring back a flagon of the waters to the court for the benefit of the king and the other knights. It would make up for his ungracious behaviour.

He rode for several days in the forest of Broceliande, without finding any trace of the fountain. One or two wayfarers and woodmen warned him that the fountain was well guarded, but they refused to tell him any more. Gawaine was only able to discover that many knights had sought the fountain, and so far none of them had returned alive. The reputation of the fountain rested on the daring of one squire who had found it and somehow escaped with a cask of healing waters. But this was many years ago, and since that day the fountain had preserved its secret. Eventually it was while resting at a lonely tavern in the depths of the forest, to which few travellers ever came, that Gawaine learnt the secret of the fountain.

An old woman, bent over a stick, grey-haired and wrinkled like a walnut, told him that the fountain belonged to a lady who was in the power of a Green Knight, and would never be released from her servitude until a Christian knight was brave enough to defeat the Green Knight and wed her.

'But if the lady is beautiful, surely she can find champions enough!' exclaimed Sir Gawaine. In his experience it was only the plain maidens who had difficulty in finding rescuers.

'Far from being beautiful, she is a witch and people say she is unbelievably hideous,' said the old lady, shaking her head. 'It is a serious matter to pledge yourself to wed a revolting witch. I am not surprised that the lady has been in bondage so long, and the Green Knight is still the tyrant of the fountain. Plenty of knights are willing to rescue her; but none of them will promise to marry her. As long as she remains unwed, the Green Knight is invincible, and the waters of the fountain will never be tasted by ordinary mortals.' Gawaine paused to reflect. It was a hard thing for a knight to marry a witch, for besides being ugly, they were a treacherous race. But his heart was moved by the tale of the Lady of the Fountain. He decided at least to attempt to rescue her, if he could do so without actually marrying her.

The old lady directed him on through the forest to the fountain. He had no difficulty in recognizing the forest clearing which she had described; but there an unpleasant surprise greeted him! The fountain was guarded, not by a Green Knight, but by a monstrous giant of a man, more like an ogre than a human being, who sat on a boulder by the spring, and leaned his huge chin on a formidable-looking club. Around him gambolled all sorts of wild beasts, whose bared fangs and menacing growls made Gawaine jump backwards. The ogre stared at Gawaine, and at last in a deep voice asked him what he wanted. Gawaine was bold enough to say straight out that he wanted to fill a flagon with the waters of the fountain, which he heard had marvellous healing powers. The ogre stared at him almost pityingly. He told him to go back before it was too late, and save his skin. He pointed to the heaps of bones and skulls which littered the clearing. They spoke for themselves. But Gawaine was not daunted. He bade the ogre stand back, and advanced resolutely towards the flowing spring. To his surprise the ogre made no attempt to stop him. But at the very moment when Gawaine was filling his flagon from the waters, a clap of thunder rent the air. The clearing darkened, and the beasts cringed at the foot of their master. Through the trees galloped a knight, dressed from head to foot in green armour.

In a second Gawaine had remounted his horse and prepared for a stern fight. But the Green Knight proved a cowardly opponent. When Gawaine showed his mettle, the Green Knight turned tail and fled at a gallop through the forest, with Gawaine in hot pursuit. A mile or so on they came on a tall castle: in a flash the Green Knight was across the drawbridge, and Gawaine was left rampaging outside. There was no sign of the knight. He had been riding up and down for about half an hour when he heard a voice calling him above his head. Looking up, he saw no one, but a gentle voice addressed him:

'Sir Knight, I am the Lady of the Fountain. You will never succeed in drinking the healing waters of the fountain, unless you release me from my enchantment.'

'How should I do that?' said Gawaine warily, remembering the old woman's warning.

'The Green Knight will never be defeated until a noble knight promises to make me his wife,' replied the lady. 'Until that day, no one will manage to defeat my oppressor.' Sir Gawaine replied that he had just put the Green Knight to flight, and saw no reason why he should not defeat him completely the next time he sallied forth from his castle. The lady told him sadly that the Green Knight's flight had been a ruse to lure him away from the fountain itself. Many a knight had been lured away, only to be beaten cruelly by the Green Knight who fought with the aid of magic. Now, Sir Gawaine had been surprised by the Green Knight's cowardice, and he believed in his heart that the lady spoke the truth.

'Am I to wed a lady whom I have never seen?' he demanded. 'That is a hard thing for any knight to do.' The lady told him sadly that this was the condition of her release. Sir Gawaine hesitated a moment: then the memory of his behaviour to Arthur came back to reproach him. He decided that he had failed his oath once, and this was his chance to redeem it by rescuing a maiden in distress, even at the cost of marrying her. In a firm voice he promised to wed the Lady of the Fountain. The lady sighed softly above his head, and threw a golden ring down from her window. She still did not show her face. She told him that the ring had magic powers and would make him invisible. The next time the Green Knight rode forth, Gawaine could slip unobserved into the castle. Sir Gawaine could not help wondering how ugly his future bride really was, and whether she looked like most witches. But he obeyed her instructions, and crept over the drawbridge when the Green Knight rode out in the morning to look for him.

To his joy he was greeted by a beautiful damsel, whose loveliness would have shone at any royal court in Britain.

75

Sir Gawaine's gallantry was well rewarded. The lady told him that she was in fact not a witch at all, but the daughter of a noble lord, who had been placed under a spell by one of her father's enemies, who wanted to get the fountain into his power. The fountain was hers, by right of inheritance, for her mother had been a water nymph who fell in love with a knight and married him. Sir Gawaine was filled with love for her, and determined to defeat the Green Knight when he returned at evening. All day they spent together in the Green Knight's castle, and Gawaine's love increased with every minute.

At sunset they heard the pounding of the Green Knight's hoofs. The lady retired to a turret and watched with fear and trembling while Sir Gawaine challenged the Green Knight to a further battle. The Green Knight clearly expected to prevail over him by magic, and dealt only very feeble blows at first. He was amazed when his magic powers had no effect on Sir Gawaine, who returned his blows with interest. In vain the Green Knight rallied all his strength to defeat Sir Gawaine. Sir Gawaine was the better fighter, and he pressed home his advantage. A few minutes of violent combat, and the Green Knight lay lifeless on the ground, with his blood staining the earth.

The Lady of the Fountain ran down and flung her arms round the neck of Sir Gawaine.

'Now I am free!' she cried joyfully. 'And my father also.' She told him that the ogre at the fountain was in fact her father, who had been put under the same enchantment. She led the knight through the forest to the bubbling spring. Sure enough, the ogre had vanished, and in his place stood an elderly knight, who stretched out his hand in eager greeting to his deliverer. The monstrous beasts had turned into the knight's faithful hounds – for the enchantment had been placed upon him while out hunting. The lady told her father that Sir Gawaine was to be her husband, and that they were returning to his native court of Camelot. Sir Conan, for that was the name of her father, decided to accompany them, and seek admittance to the fellowship of the Round Table.

Thus Sir Gawaine returned in triumph to Arthur's court, having won himself a beautiful bride, and vindicated his oath. Once before the king, he begged his pardon humbly for having offended him by his boorish behaviour. Then he laid at his feet a flagon of the fountain's waters as an atonement.

'I hope this means that Gawaine has conquered his jealousy,' thought Arthur. 'He could be the greatest of my knights. There is so much good in him. But his fatal pride warps it all. Let us hope he will control it in the future. Perhaps Mordred will help him to overcome it. Mordred is always so respectful and polite, and he could teach Gawaine many things.'

Arthur's words were truer than he knew. Mordred could indeed teach Gawaine many things. But because Mordred's nature was evil, it would have been better for Arthur and the Round Table if Gawaine had never learned them.

8

SIR TRISTRAM
TO THE RESCUE

*I*n a castle on the rocky coast of Cornwall a furious squire stormed at his king:

'You have used me unjustly, my liege, by the Rood I swear it! I have served you faithfully for many years, and yet you will not knight me.'

King Mark of Cornwall cowered from the anger of Tristram, the elder brother of Bors and Balin. He was nearly a foot taller than the wizened king. Tristram's eyes flashed with fury as he recalled the wrongs which he had endured in order to win his spurs from this cowardly ruler. King Mark had one ruling passion – money. His heart lay in his money bags. He never sent his knights on an adventure, if he thought it would cost him a penny. He never gave banquets or held tournaments.

Now he faced the unpleasant prospect of knighting his squire, and having to engage another one. Another mouth to feed. As for armour and equipment – he writhed at the idea. But Tristram would not be put off.

'Either you knight me at once, or else I abandon you for the court of King Arthur, where my brother Sir Balin is held in high esteem.' King Mark searched frantically round for some way out. He had lately decided that he must marry. But he recoiled at the prospect of wooing a princess for himself, and the expense of a long courtship. He had selected the Princess Iseult, daughter of an Irish king, as the most suitable bride. Supposing he sent Tristram to Ireland to woo the girl, and spare himself unpleasantness and expense.

King Mark promised to knight him there and then on the spot if he would only woo the Princess Iseult by proxy. Tristram despised himself for his weakness in not standing out against Mark.

On the voyage to Ireland, Tristram struck up a great friendship with the captain of the ship. By the time the boat lay off the coast of Ireland, he had taught Tristram to be as good a sailor as anyone else on board. Each swore to help the other should they fall into danger in the future.

Tristram journeyed inland towards the court of King Dermot, father of the Princess Iseult. On his way he learned that seven kings and five princes had sought her hand in marriage, but the Princess Iseult had rejected them all because she did not love them.

Tristram found Ireland wild and uninhabited compared to the sunny land of Cornwall. Huge lakes stretched out among the lonely hills; hermits dwelt in caves among the rocks, who probably never spoke to more than ten human beings during the year. It was while riding through one of these deserted places, in a narrow gorge between two lowering crags, that a knight drew out from behind a boulder and challenged Tristram.

'I am Tristram of Brittany and Cornwall. No man bars me from the path I wish to take.' The stranger did not answer Tristram's brave words: he merely aimed a vigorous blow at Tristram's shield, which sent Tristram staggering back. With his visor down, it was impossible to tell who it was, and Tristram had no idea why he had been attacked. But he was not the man to accept a blow lying down: he flew at his opponent, and dealt blow upon blow at him. After many minutes of silent, remorseless conflict, the enemy seemed to weaken. Tristram summoned all his strength and pierced his opponent's armour with his lance. The knight fell to the ground with a cry and lay there dead. Sadly Tristram dragged the body to the roadside and gazed down at his handiwork. It had not been his wish to kill this unknown knight.

Tristram remounted his horse and rode on through the causeway. Several hundred yards farther, he found the explanation for the stranger's sudden attack. The dead bodies of two unarmed men lay on the roadside. Beside them were piles of jewels and gold, which had evidently been stripped from them. Tristram knew now that he had probably rid the world of a worthless robber knight.

A week later, he reached the court of King Dermot, which lay in the far south of Ireland, not far from the famous lakes of Killarney. He looked forward to a hearty welcome at the Irish court. To his disappointment the court was in heavy mourning, for the king's only son, Sir Marhaus, had been foully murdered by a robber who had escaped from the scene of the crime too quickly for the king's men to catch him and hang him. The king's nephew, Sir Blamor, who was now the heir to the throne, had vowed at the high altar to wipe out the cruel deed with the blood of the murderer. For several weeks Tristram was compelled to put off his ceremonial visit to the Princess Iseult for she was overcome with grief and could not receive anyone.

Iseult's first sight of Tristram was at a tournament, to which she had come listlessly and reluctantly, at the instigation of her faithful maid Bragwine, who pointed out the foreigner from Cornwall, and Iseult's interest was aroused. Tristram's prowess proclaimed him of noble if not royal birth, and she wondered what had brought him to the south of Ireland. Modest as she was, it crossed her mind that Tristram might possibly have come to her father's court to see her famous beauty for himself. At the evening's banquet, Iseult smiled graciously upon Tristram and complimented him upon his success in the tournament. Tristram kissed her hand in homage and vowed that her presence had inspired him.

It was only natural that these two young and good-looking people should take pleasure in each other's company. Tristram's skill at archery outshone that of all the Irishmen, and his swordplay was equally good. Iseult delighted to learn how to draw a bow with him, and many happy hours were passed in the garden of the castle, where Iseult had a miniature target put up. Bragwine knew Iseult too well not to notice the signs of love in her behaviour. But Tristram spoke no word of actual love, nor gazed at Iseult with rapture. Bragwine's sentimental heart worried over the problem.

The Feast of St. Patrick, the greatest festival in Ireland, was always celebrated at the court of King Dermot by a great tournament, to which knights came from the farther corners of the realm, and even from the coast of Wales. As Tristram rode into the lists, the Princess Iseult beckoned to him, and pinned her favour, a fluttering white ribbon, on to his helmet. Many of the courtiers marked the gesture and gossiped among themselves that they would soon be losing their fair princess. Sir Tristram acquitted himself well, and it was carelessness rather than lack of skill which allowed Sir Blamor to wound him in the arm. The wound went deep, and Sir Tristram turned faint through loss of blood. To the horror of the princess, he swayed in the saddle, and fell from his horse. Instantly Iseult ordered him to be borne to her tent.

It was some hours later that Sir Blamor made his way to the tent, eager to ask how Tristram was, and beg his pardon for the wound. As he gazed in remorse at the knight's pale face, his attention was caught by Tristram's lance. He noticed that the tip of it was missing. Sir Blamor's face darkened horribly when he saw it. Without another word he took a small piece of steel from his pocket and compared it with the lance. It fitted exactly! Sir Blamor rushed to the council chamber of the king.

'My lord!' he gasped, 'there is a traitor and a murderer lying here in our midst!'

'A traitor?' exclaimed the king, starting from his chair in surprise. 'Let him be seized and brought before me.'

'Suppose he were an honoured guest?' demanded Sir Blamor vehemently. 'And suppose all the time this man was in fact the murderer of Sir Marhaus, your only son?' Iseult had followed Blamor into the hall, in time to hear his last words.

'Name this murderer, this slayer of our innocent son!' cried the king in a loud voice. Sir Blamor flourished the lance in the air, and fitted into it the piece of steel from his pocket.

'Behold the lance of Sir Tristram,' he shouted, 'and behold the piece of steel which was drawn from the wound which slew the noble Sir Marhaus. See how the two fit!

There is no room for doubt that Tristram is the murderer.'
The king's first instinct was to have Tristram killed where
he lay. But Sir Blamor persuaded him that the right of
vengeance belonged to him, and that in any case it would
not be fitting to avenge Marhaus' death by another foul
crime.

'Let the murderer recover from his wounds, and then I
will challenge him to mortal combat,' said Sir Blamor
proudly. 'God will defend the right, and see that justice is
done.' King Dermot agreed reluctantly that Blamor's
plan was the right one. Tristram was to be guarded night
and day until he had recovered enough to meet Blamor's
challenge.

Late that night, however, Bragwine stole through the
curtains of Sir Tristram's tent, and pressed a flagon of
drugged wine upon the sleepy guard. Then she beckoned
to Iseult, who flung herself down beside Sir Tristram's
couch and besought him to take the chance to escape.
Weakened by his wound, it took some time for Tristram to
grasp what she was saying. When he understood that he
was believed to be the murderer of Sir Marhaus, his anger
knew no bounds. He realized that Sir Marhaus, the idol of
the court, had been in secret a robber knight of the most
despicable kind whom he had slain after a fair fight.

'Do you believe I slew your brother unfairly?' he asked
Iseult in a fierce whisper. Iseult buried her face in her
hands.

'I do not know what to believe,' she sobbed. 'All my life
I have honoured my cousin Blamor. Why should he lie to
me now?'

Tristram's stern face softened. He told her how
Marhaus had met his death, and how he had discovered

the corpses of Marhaus' victims on the road, proving how Marhaus had made a living in secret. Then Iseult recalled how many times Marhaus had given her rich jewels for her birthday, which must have cost far more than he could afford. She begged Sir Tristram's pardon for her disbelief, and promised to do all she could to help him recover for the fight with Sir Blamor. For Sir Tristram pointed out that only thus would he wipe out the fearful stain on his honour; if he escaped it would seem like an admission of guilt.

Cured by Iseult's healing potions, it was not long before Sir Blamor judged him fit enough to ride his horse into the lists, and answer for Marhaus' murder.

The crowd was hostile to Sir Tristram from the first, for news of his guilt had been spread by the guards and courtiers. Sir Blamor, on the other hand, was greeted with cheers and acclamations. He too looked grim and determined, as he rode by: for he had seen that the white pennant still fluttered from Tristram's helmet, and since he, too, loved the Princess Iseult, jealousy, as well as revenge, inspired him. Iseult, in the royal box, had rouged her cheeks lest she betrayed her fear for Sir Tristram, who was still weak.

Indeed, at first the fight went all Sir Blamor's way, and Iseult was hard put to it not to scream in agony as the blows rained upon Sir Tristram. But savage determination to prove his innocence supported Tristram. In spite of more wounds, and the reopening of his old one, he returned blow for blow, and seemed to gather fresh strength as he fought. It was Blamor now who weakened and quailed before Tristram's charge. It was Blamor who reined in his horse and tried to protect himself with his shield. At length Blamor's arm bent beneath Tristram's blows, and it was he who crashed heavily to the ground amid universal groans of dismay and fury. At that moment Tristram's life was in more danger than ever it had been during the fight: the wild onlookers would have rushed upon him and torn him limb by limb in their rage, but Iseult plucked at her father's sleeve in anguish and cried:

'Show yourself a king, my lord, and assert yourself over these howling assassins. Sir Tristram has proved his innocence in the eyes of God and men by defeating Sir Blamor. Do not stain your royal honour by allowing these barbarians to tear him to pieces!' Iseult's brave words stung the king to action. He ordered his squires to rescue Tristram and bear him into the castle. Tristram was half dead when they reached him, but he rallied in time to demand to be borne before the king.

Then, in a low clear voice, he told the true story of Marhaus' death, as it had happened in the lonely hills. Before he had finished speaking, two young knights came forward, boyhood friends of Marhaus, who confirmed his sad tale. They had known how Marhaus spent his days, and had not dared to tell the king, for fear of Marhaus' revenge. Now they dared to tell King Dermot to his face that his only son had been a robber and a murderer. King Dermot begged Tristram's pardon in a voice which could scarcely be heard, so choked was it with unhappiness. Supported by his squires, Sir Blamor staggered up to the royal box, and fell before Sir Tristram; he, too, begged his pardon and asked what the royal house of Ireland could do to atone for their treatment of Sir Tristram.

'Let me grant you some favour,' begged the king, 'that I

may prove to you how sorely I repent my behaviour.' Tristram looked grave: 'Let me spend one more month at your court, and then I will name my request and leave you for ever.'

'It shall be so,' answered the king solemnly. 'I swear to grant whatever you shall demand in one month from now.' He and all his courtiers felt in no doubt that Tristram would ask for Iseult's hand in marriage.

Every day Tristram rode with the princess, and spoke to her of Cornwall, and his life there. He enchanted her with descriptions of the beautiful countryside, the long hours of sunshine, so different from the damp climate of Ireland. Iseult felt that she would be glad to exchange Ireland for Cornwall as the bride of Sir Tristram. Tristram never ceased to talk to her of King Mark and the kingdom of Cornwall. Iseult sometimes felt that she knew more about the king than about the knight, but she was so happy in her love for Tristram that she did not complain. On the twenty-eighth day after Tristram's fight with Blamor, she arrayed herself in a shining robe, and placed her royal coronet upon her head. Smiling radiantly, she took her royal place beside her father as Tristram strode through the council chamber and knelt before the king.

King Dermot smiled encouragingly. 'I think we can all guess what our guest will ask,' he said, 'and I will say in advance that nothing would give more pleasure than to grant his wish.' Tristram's face gave nothing away.

'Will King Dermot really grant me anything I ask?' King Dermot took this to be a mere formality. He nodded eagerly. Tristram did not look at Iseult. He hated what he had to do but Iseult would have to be sacrificed on the altar of his honour.

'I ask for the hand of the Princess Iseult for my master, King Mark of Cornwall,' said Tristram in a loud, firm voice. He looked King Dermot straight in the eyes as he spoke, daring him to refuse. Dermot turned pale, then red. His hand strayed to the hilt of his sword. Was this a deliberate insult to his daughter? Sir Blamor restrained him.

'You have given your royal word to the treacherous dog,' he said in a fierce whisper. 'Do not add crime to crime. The name of Dermot of Ireland must not stink in the nostrils of honourable men.' Dermot controlled himself with a visible effort.

'Is it *possible* that you should ask this?' he said in a low trembling voice.

'I ask it. That is enough,' was all Tristram would reply.

'More than enough,' broke in Sir Blamor. 'You will be granted your boon. Now get out of our sight, and do not offend our gaze until the day of your departure. You have won the affections of our beloved Iseult, and now you cast her aside, and throw her into the arms of your master. I would that the rules of hospitality allowed me to treat you as I would like – not with a sword this time, but a horse-whip.' Sir Tristram bore Sir Blamor's reproaches in silence. He turned on his heel and left them.

All this time Iseult had said nothing. She stared straight ahead of her, with the tears falling down her cheeks.

Iseult would neither eat nor drink in the days before her departure. King Dermot could not bear the idea of his daughter condemned to a loveless marriage. He sent for Bragwine. The two conspirators whispered together for an hour or so. Then the maid left the king and went on a secret errand to the marshes outside the town.

When the time came for Iseult to board the ship, Dermot pleaded with Tristram to allow her to have her maid with her. Tristram gave in and Bragwine crept aboard, carrying a small pitcher under her cloak, the love potion she had fetched from the witch of the marshes.

Once they had set sail, Tristram kept himself severely apart. He had no wish to encourage Iseult in her grief by visiting her. Besides, her tears and illness reproached him more than he liked to admit. Tristram was not in love with Iseult. From the first he had recognized the fact that she was to be the bride of his master, and had schooled himself to look on her beauty and grace with proper detachment. On the other hand, he knew King Mark's true nature only too well. To what sort of life was he condemning this innocent girl? And all for the sake of his knightly promise. If the rules of chivalry had not been ingrained in Sir Tristram, he would have left Iseult in Ireland and scorned the consequences.

Bragwine watched him every day. She saw his frowns and his angry sighs. They convinced her that Tristram was pining for love of her mistress. Why should she use the love potion to make Iseult fall in love with King Mark?

One evening she came up to Tristram and asked him if he would honour her mistress by drinking a glass of wine with her.

'I thank the Princess Iseult,' replied Tristram, 'but it is late, and it would be better for her to get some rest.' Bragwine persisted until he weakened. Tristram went below and greeted Iseult. He tried not to notice her pallor and the dark circles under her eyes. He assured her that he had never seen her looking more beautiful; Iseult gave him a sad little smile.

Together they lifted the rich goblets and drank a solemn toast to the voyage. Scarcely had Tristram tasted the wine, than his mouth, throat and stomach started to burn as if he had swallowed a glass of liquid fire. He dashed the goblet to the ground and sprang to his feet.

'What poison is this?' he cried. 'Are you trying to get your revenge on me this way?' Iseult was dumbfounded by his anger.

'That is my father's best wine,' she replied haughtily. 'It was his parting present to me. The taste is mellow and gentle, and you have often admired it in the old days.' But Tristram was no longer listening, he flung himself on his knees.

'Iseult! Oh, fairest of princesses!' he said. 'I cannot take you to King Mark and see you married to another man. Flesh and blood cannot endure it. Such love burns in me, that I feel as if I am on fire with it.' Tristram gazed at Iseult as ardently as the most lovesick girl could have wished. The lovers fell into each other's arms, and abandoned all the restraint which had kept them apart. For the rest of the journey, Iseult was in the seventh heaven of happiness. She spent every minute of the day with her beloved, and grudged the hours of sleep which kept them apart. When they reached the coast of Cornwall, Iseult asked Tristram what was to be their future.

'Surely it was God who revealed my love to me!' exclaimed Sir Tristram. 'Otherwise, why should I have fallen so suddenly and so passionately in love with you, when I had resisted your charms for so long. I cannot believe that I am meant to take you to the court and deliver you to the king.' Tristram told Iseult to spend the

89

night at a convent near by, while he was deciding what to do next. Tristram was awakened early by his own squire Governale, who had joined him at the port. Governale told him that Bragwine was lying between life and death and was calling urgently for Sir Tristram. Tristram went to her. She pressed his hand and whispered hoarsely:

'Forgive me, noble knight, for I did it for the best.'

'Surely you have done nothing that I need to forgive!' he said gently. Then Bragwine made her sad confession. With her last breath, she begged Tristram's forgiveness for her deception.

'I did it for her, for the princess,' she gasped.

'Alas, Bragwine,' said Sir Tristram sadly, 'what mischief you did with that potion. How much better if you had kept it for your mistress and King Mark. I know not how long it will take to undo the harm which you have caused.'

For now all Tristram's scruples had returned.

'It is my duty to give up Iseult,' he thought. 'No matter what it costs us, we must do our duty.' He went straightway to the convent where Iseult was resting. Iseult could not believe that Tristram was going to desert her again. She began to think that some evil fate dogged her. In vain Tristram begged her to take comfort from the memory of their love. She flung herself at Tristram's feet, begging and imploring him to marry her. All her tears and entreaties could not swerve Tristram's firm intention. At last Iseult wore herself out with her sorrow and she fell backwards in a trance, not knowing or caring what became of her. When the news was brought of Bragwine's death, Iseult said not a word, but the tears flowed freely down her cheeks.

'Oh, would that she had never tried to help me!' she thought. 'I know that I shall never love another man as I love Sir Tristram.'

The next day Iseult was borne towards the royal court of Cornwall in a magnificent litter which King Mark had borrowed and sent to fetch her. Sir Tristram rode beside her, but never a word passed between them during the whole journey.

With great dignity Iseult alighted from her litter and allowed herself to be led into the great hall of the castle by Sir Tristram. The hand which held hers was burning hot.

'My liege of Cornwall,' said Tristram, with a low bow, 'I present to you the Princess Iseult of Ireland, your affianced bride.' Iseult swept a low curtsy.

'And now I take my leave of you for ever,' continued Sir Tristram, levelly. King Mark started up.

'B-but what's the matter?' he cried. 'Are you mad, Tristram? I depend on you, you must not do this. Look, I will give you money, yes, I will even do that. Only don't leave me, Tristram.' Tristram cut short his terrified protests.

'You will have to find someone else. I am going to the court of the Round Table, to enter the service of King Arthur. I can no longer serve a master whom I *despise*!' Mark cowered back. He did not dare move while Tristram gave him a contemptuous nod of the head, and strode out of the hall without a backward glance at Iseult.

'I shall never see him again,' thought Iseult.

SIR TRISTRAM TO THE RESCUE

On the Feast of All Saints King Arthur surveyed the full

panoply of his knights. The court was rejoicing and making merry; only one knight sat sunk in gloom.

King Arthur sighed. Sir Tristram had been like this since his arrival at court. He was courageous to the point of recklessness in battle, but the moment the excitement of the fight left him, he became moody and morose. Sir Tristram had not confided his sad story to any of his new comrades, not even his own brother, Sir Balin.

A commotion in the hall distracted Arthur's attention from Sir Tristram. There were shouts of 'Spy! Spy!' and 'Traitor!' After a good deal of scuffling, a young man was dragged before the king, held down by four or five men-at-arms.

'We can tell from his speech that he is Cornish,' said one of the soldiers who was holding his arms behind his back. 'And we all know how to treat Cornish spies.' Since King Mark still refused to take the oath of allegiance to Arthur, the Cornish were extremely unpopular in Camelot.

'I am no spy,' said the youth indignantly. 'My name is Governale, and I am of noble birth. I have come here on an important mission, and I will not be handled thus. Lay off me, you fellows, else you will feel the point of my sword.'

'Peace,' said Arthur sternly, 'and have the goodness to keep your weapon sheathed in this hall. Now tell us what your mission is, and what has brought you to the court.'

'I bear a message from Queen Iseult of Cornwall to Sir Tristram.' The words rang out clearly through the hall. At the sound of the name 'Iseult', Sir Tristram started violently from his reverie and looked wildly round. He leaped from his seat and ran towards the stranger, crying:

'Governale! What news of her?' The knights of the

Round Table did not fail to notice Sir Tristram's frantic expression, so different from his usual look of apathetic sadness.

'Alas, my lord,' replied Governale, kissing Tristram's hand. 'Grievous tidings. I scarcely know how to tell you what has happened at the ill-fated court of Cornwall.'

'Tell me, tell me,' cried Sir Tristram. 'Do not keep me in agonies, Governale.'

Then Governale unfolded his sad tale. The ill-famed Moors of Spain, who roamed the seas for plunder and had won themselves a name for cruelty, had attacked Cornwall. The onslaught of the Moors was only feebly resisted by King Mark and his knights. A short, fierce battle on the foreshore, and King Mark's army was in flight for the castle, while the beach was strewn with corpses. A few hours later, and the castle itself was in Moorish hands, with every man in it, from the king to the lowest pantry boy, a prisoner.

King Mark begged for mercy, heedless of the traditions of chivalry, by which a true knight never grovels to his opponent in the hopes of getting a lighter punishment. The Moorish leader beckoned to one of his servitors, a pale-skinned boy. He gave a string of orders to the lad, who turned and addressed King Mark thus:

'Palomedes of Spain and Morocco greets Mark of Cornwall. Palomedes has no wish to harm the King of Cornwall. If the king agrees to what Palomedes demands, neither he nor any of his knights will regret it.' Mark was astonished at the boy's faultless accent.

'You are no Moor,' he cried in surprise, 'but a Christian like ourselves. Are you not ashamed to serve a pagan master?' The boy frowned and glanced at Palomedes.

93

'My birth is as good as yours, Mark of Cornwall, for I am a king's son. Palomedes captured me when I was a child, from the palace which was my home. He killed my four brothers, but me he adopted and had brought up at his own court, for he wanted to have an interpreter to deal with the conquered Christians whom he ground under his heel.'

'Have you no wish to escape?' cried Mark. 'No longing for a life among your own people?'

'Who are my people?' demanded the boy Lothar sadly. 'The Christians who share my blood, or the Moors who have shared my life since the age of five? What Christian knight would own me now, after so long in the hands of his mortal enemies. No, Mark, this is my destiny. I shall act as the interpreter of Palomedes so long as he requires me, and then perhaps retire into some monastery and end my days at least among Christians.'

Mark begged the boy to intercede with Palomedes for him. 'No, he will take from you all your gold and jewels,' said the boy, 'leaving you only enough to buy food for seven days. Furthermore, you must pay an enormous ransom for the leading knight in your realm, whom Palomedes will hold as a hostage in Spain.' As Lothar finished dictating the Moor's terms, the Queen Iseult, pale and listless as usual, was seen to walk on the terrace outside the castle. The Moor's black eyes regarded her with delight, and he whispered something to Lothar. Lothar ordered Mark to have her fetched before Palomedes. Iseult retained all her queenly dignity in the presence of the Moor, and looked him bravely in the eyes.

The Moor was obviously greatly impressed by her beauty. He gave another order to Lothar, who turned pale, and argued with him. The Moor would not be contradicted: he growled at his interpreter, and made as if to strike him. Hastily, Lothar turned once more to Mark and began:

'The beauty of your queen has found favour with my master Palomedes. He will take the fair Iseult as his hostage, and leave your knights in peace.' Mark actually rejoiced to hear that he himself was to come to no harm. He allowed Iseult to be bound with silken ropes and taken aboard Palomedes' own ship, promising to find the money for her ransom as soon as possible. In her heart of hearts, Iseult wondered if Mark would ever consent to ransom her for the amount of money which Palomedes demanded. But Governale, who had lurked on the seashore when the Moors embarked with their booty, managed to bring a smile to her pale lips when he whispered:

'Take courage, fair queen. I will straightway ride to my master Tristram, at the court of King Arthur, and enlist his aid. He will rescue you from the Moors if anyone can.'

When Governale's story ended, Tristram swore a great oath which echoed through the hall.

'I shall rescue the Queen Iseult, if it cost me my life! I swear it,' he cried. Forthwith he rode out from Camelot, with the blessing of King Arthur upon him. In Cornwall he bearded King Mark and asked him what steps he was taking to ransom the queen.

'Is she not your wife?' he shouted in a voice which made Mark cringe.

'They say this Palomedes is not such a bad fellow,' replied Mark. 'Besides, he was greatly impressed by the queen's beauty, and I have no doubt he will shower favours upon her. We are probably doing her a service by letting her spend a couple of years at his court, until I have collected the ransom.'

At these words, Sir Tristram, forgetting his oath of loyalty to the king, smote him violently to the ground and blazed out at him:

'You are not worthy to wear your father's crown. I myself will rescue the Queen Iseult with my own true sword. Since you will thus save the sum of her ransom, you must promise me something in return.' Mark cowered before the knight's fury, and promised him anything he should ask.

'If I rescue Iseult,' cried Sir Tristram, 'you must take the oath of allegiance to Arthur of Camelot. In this way your miserable people will at least have a proper man as an overlord, even if their king is a wretched worm.' Tristram spurned the king contemptuously with his mailed foot, and strode out of the hall.

Tristram's impetuous rush from the castle was barred by a familiar figure. His old comrade, the sea-captain, put his hand on his arm and said calmly:

'I think you have need of me, my friend. Rumour has it that you are about to set off on a wild-goose chase to Spain.'

'Rumour is correct,' said Sir Tristram, curtly. 'I am off to rescue your Queen Iseult. But if you call that a wild-goose chase, I warn you I shall treat you as I have just treated your king.' The sea-captain smiled.

'I was always one for wild-goose chases,' he said, 'and I have a whim to set sail for Spain again. I know the coast, and can help you. We can embark for the land of the Moors this very night, for the tide will favour us.' Tristram accepted his offer joyfully.

At last the rocky coast of Spain began to take shape on the horizon. It was in both their minds that Tristram might never return from his dangerous mission; but neither put the thought into words. They planned to meet in a lonely cove on a certain day.

With a last farewell, Tristram quitted the boat and scrambled up the steep cliffs which fringed the coast.

He travelled on and learnt from an innkeeper that Palomedes' stronghold was many leagues to the south, in the heart of the Moorish kingdom. He learnt, too, that no Moorish chief was more dreaded than Iseult's captor, who had won himself a legendary reputation for ferocity and invincibility.

'They say,' muttered the innkeeper, 'that Palomedes has lately captured a fair Christian lady from far-off Britain, of whom he is much enamoured.'

'A Christian lady?' Tristram inquired casually. 'And is she enamoured of the Moor?'

'On the contrary,' replied the innkeeper. 'Men say she will have nothing to do with him, but remains all day in her room and weeps all day for her native Britain. Palomedes is rumoured to have given her until Christmas to decide her fate, and after that he will hurl her into the deepest dungeon, if she rejects him.' Tristram's anger boiled up at this news of Palomedes' treachery: for it was an established rule that no hostage held for ransom should be ill-treated or threatened with dire penalties. He realized that Palomedes had no intention of releasing Iseult even if King Mark scraped together the ransom money.

He thanked the innkeeper and asked him boldly if he favoured the Christian cause. The innkeeper looked him up and down. He liked what he saw.

97

'I would not say a word against Palomedes and the Moors,' said the innkeeper with a faint smile, 'because I do not know who may be listening to us. I will say this: if you ever need help, call on me.' Tristram asked him for a horse and armour and set off for Palomedes' stronghold with more confidence in his heart.

By the time he reached the small market town, which was dominated by Palomedes' menacing castle, it was only a few days before Christmas. Not knowing where to lodge, Tristram took the desperate course of following a young girl to her home, judging from her white skin that she had no Moorish blood.

'Let me be!' she cried in Spanish, as Tristram took her arm.

'Do not fear,' replied Tristram, 'for I mean you no harm. Let me enter your house with you and explain my predicament.' The girl tossed back her black hair and nodded sullenly, as if she cared not whether Tristram came or went. She led him into a small dark room, lit only by the firelight, which glimmered against the bare walls. An old man crouched over the fire. He did not stir or look up when Tristram entered.

'Speak now,' said the Spanish girl, folding her arms akimbo and gazing at him sternly. Tristram told her that he was a Christian knight who wanted a refuge where he might hide from the Moorish soldiers until he had accomplished a certain mission.

'Tell me more about your mission,' said the girl suspiciously.

'Are you for or against the Moors?' countered Tristram boldly. The girl led him over to the fireplace and pointed mutely at the old man, whose face was lit up by the flames.

Tristram started back in horror: for the old man's eyes were sightless!

'That is your answer,' she said passionately. 'See what the Moors did to my grandfather because he stood up for his faith in front of them, and refused to embrace their pagan religion. My grandfather was the leading citizen of this town; we lived in a fine house; round my neck hung the finest jewels you could find in the South of Spain. Now, we live in this hovel which one of our former servants found for us.' Tristram's pity was aroused by the girl's anguish.

'There is more to life than silks and jewels and fine horses and a big house,' he said gently. Isabella gazed at him, and her eyes filled with tears.

'I could forgive Palomedes all this,' she replied, 'if he had not slain my lover, Don Diego. Diego was the finest knight in all the world, and his faithful heart burned with anger at our misfortunes. He challenged the Moor to a fair fight, and before all the town that cruel tyrant slew him.' Tristram confided his own sad story and asked her what chance he had of rescuing the Queen Iseult if Palomedes might be willing to answer another Christian challenge. Isabella wept anew and begged him not to get himself killed. She told him that Palomedes' fame as a fighter outstripped that of even the greatest Christian knights, and that his powerful physique, combined with his superb horses made him an invincible opponent.

Sir Tristram replied proudly that the Knights of the Round Table were not afraid to meet the devil himself, armed with a shield of fire. He wrapped himself in Don Diego's thick cloak and set off to explore the town and, if possible, the castle.

Unseen by Isabella, a Turkish ruffian, who was one of Palomedes' crew of body-servants, was watching her cottage. He had fallen a victim to Isabella's beauty, and desired to have her for his own. When he saw another man leave the cottage, his rage and jealousy knew no bounds. He hastened to his master, Palomedes, and reported that he had seen a spy leave the house of Isabella. Palomedes smiled wickedly.

'Let's have this spy up at my castle,' said he, 'and see what he has discovered from the beautiful Isabella, beyond the fact that she has a comely figure and a fine pair of eyes. Go fetch this man, you Turk, and see that he comes to no harm until he reaches me.' The warning was necessary, for the Turk delighted to manhandle his powerless prisoners. Tristram was taken completely by surprise when four stout Moorish soldiers seized his arms and pinioned him securely. In vain he shouted to the crowd in the market place to rescue him; the Christians were too cowed to resist.

'Get word to Isabella,' shouted Sir Tristram as he was borne away struggling. One lad had enough courage to take his message to Isabella. She determined to get inside the castle.

Meanwhile, Sir Tristram was being dragged before Palomedes himself. The Moorish chief quickly recognized Tristram for what he was. His curiosity was aroused. What could have brought a noble knight so far afield? Something about Tristram's speech puzzled Palomedes. He called Lothar to him and asked what land his captive came from.

'By his accent I would say he came from Cornwall,' replied Lothar. The pagan warrior's eyes gleamed with pleasure. He had solved the mystery! His prisoner had come to Spain to rescue Iseult, and the heartless pagan saw a neat way of amusing himself at the expense of his captive. He ordered Lothar to fetch the lady Iseult, and when she was brought before him, pale and worn with suffering, he pointed cruelly to the helpless figure of Tristram.

'Here is an old acquaintance for you, to while away your imprisonment,' said Palomedes. He noticed the convulsive shudder which shook Iseult's whole frame when she saw Tristram; and he wondered what relationship these two had to each other. As for Tristram, his despair could not be hidden at the sight of his beloved Iseult. He strained his bonds and struggled with his captors, until it looked as if he would break free from six of the stoutest Moors, despite the ropes which bound him.

'How do you find the lady Iseult?' continued Palomedes, deliberately baiting Tristram. 'Is she not looking beautiful? I think her paleness suits her. She will make a lovely bride on Christmas Day.'

'Never, while I live!' muttered Tristram. Palomedes questioned Tristram further about his native land, and his loyalty to the king of Cornwall, and he asked him several times if he thought it right to love the wife of another man. Tristram refused to answer this offensive question; he replied proudly that his oath as a Knight of the Round Table bound him to rescue a lady in distress.

'The Round Table!' cried Palomedes excitedly. 'Ah, I have always longed to meet one of that gallant fellowship. Now I will pit my strength against one of Arthur Pendragon's knights, and show the world which is the better fighter.' Palomedes ordered Tristram to be mounted forthwith on one of his best horses, and attired in the pagan's second-best suit of armour. He was determined that no one should reproach him for having defeated one of the famous Knights of the Round Table unfairly. Tristram was amazed, for he did not know the great reputation which the Round Table had acquired as far abroad as Spain and Italy, and even Morocco, Palomedes' native land. He asked the Moor what inducement he would give him to take part in this fight. Palomedes paused to consider and then remarked carelessly:

'Your fate is sealed, Christian knight, for Palomedes has never yet been defeated in battle. But if you fight well and sell your life dearly, it is possible I shall release the lady Iseult when her ransom comes.' Then Tristram's heart was filled with despair, for he knew that it might be ten years before King Mark consented to part with the enormous ransom which had been asked.

'And if Palomedes is defeated?' he cried recklessly. The Moor's face darkened. 'That shall never be,' he replied angrily. 'But if Allah wills that I fall before a Christian lance, rest assured that my men will fall upon you and kill you like the Christian dog you are.' Reflecting that he was bound to die anyway, Tristram resolved grimly to sell his life as dearly as possible, and concentrate his last hours on earth encompassing the rescue of Iseult. Fortune favoured him, for as he was being dragged from the hall, Lothar edged up beside him and whispered:

'Palomedes has ordered the lady Iseult to be set on a horse, and brought to the scene of the battle, so that she may witness the downfall of her champion. I am to guard her, for he trusts me. But since I set eyes on the Cornish queen, my heart has been filled with love for her, and I would willingly rescue her at the cost of my own life. Therefore at the moment when Palomedes slays you, I shall spur my horse, and set off with her at a gallop in a desperate bid for freedom.'

Never had a Knight of the Round Table faced such fearful odds as did Sir Tristram when he rode to face Palomedes. Ranks of Moorish soldiers watched him, and their gleaming swords reminded him of his inevitable fate, supposing he had the good luck to defeat his adversary. He inclined low before the queen, as she sat motionless on her palfrey. Both knew it might be the last time they gazed at each other on earth.

Then he faced the Moor proudly and spurred his horse to a gallop, prepared to conquer or die in the attempt. Palomedes fought with the mastery of an experienced warrior, the hero of a hundred victories. But Sir Tristram fought with the desperation of a man who has nothing to lose; every blow of his lance on the Moor's shield seemed to have the strength of ten men behind it. His fierce charges shook the ground with their violence, and the thunder of his horse's hoofs might have been heard as far away as Gibraltar. The noise reached the ears of Isabella as she toiled towards the castle; when she saw the fight in progress, her first thought was that it was too late, and that Sir Tristram would meet the same fate as Don Diego. But like Sir Tristram, despair gave her new courage. Seeing Lothar beside Iseult, with the Turk in close attendance, she sidled up to them and smiled winningly at the lovesick Turk.

The Turk's attention was distracted at the very moment when Tristram was piercing Palomedes through and through with his sword. The two champions had abandoned their chargers. It was as two equal swordsmen that the final battle between Moor and Christian was fought out. Palomedes reeled back beneath the blinding pain of Tristram's sword in his breast, and fell to the ground with a hideous gurgling cry which curdled the blood of all the spectators. Only a moment of distraction, only one minute in which the Turk gazed lovingly at the Spanish girl and failed to see the desperate straits of his master! But it was enough for Lothar to whip up Iseult's horse and spur his own to a mighty gallop. Sir Tristram remounted his charger, and leaping the dying body of the Moor, followed them down the hill at a pace which sent the dust flying. With a cry of rage the Turk flung Isabella aside, and shouted to the Moorish soldiers to set off in pursuit. The body of Palomedes lay neglected on the grass, while the Moorish cavalry dashed after the fugitives.

There was no time for words between Tristram and Iseult. When the queen's palfrey began to tire, the knight caught her up into his own saddle, and the two rode forward together. How relieved they were to reach the tavern of the friendly innkeeper!

'A knight in armour, a fair lady and a squire,' murmured the innkeeper. 'Yes, you fit the description well.' He told Tristram that, although they had out-distanced their pursuers, the Moors were determined to revenge Palomedes' death. All the ports were being watched, and the Moorish fleet was held in readiness to pursue any unlawful boat which left the shores of Spain. Meanwhile, all the taverners had been given a description of the fugitives, and a huge reward had been promised. To

Tristram's grief, he told them that the Turk had plunged his dagger into Isabella's breast for her part in the affair.

The innkeeper kept his word to Tristram and hid the fugitives in the straw of his barn. It was in the middle of the night that the three were awakened by the sound of horses' hoofs, and hoarse cries of Moorish soldiers. Tristram pulled the heaps of straw about their heads and bade Lothar and Iseult keep complete silence. They listened to the innkeeper protesting all the time that he had been wakened from his sleep on a fool's errand. But the soldiers would not be deflected from searching the house and outbuildings. A quarter of an hour later the barn loft shook as heavy mailed feet tramped up the steps. The Moorish captain looked round the derelict barn with disgust. He turned on his heel, barking an order over his shoulder. The next thing Tristram knew, a sharp sword was probing the straw above their heads. He pressed Iseult's hand. All three held their breath. As the last sound of the soldiers died away, Tristram heaved a sigh of relief and whispered:

'That was a near escape. Thank God that the soldier did not do his job more efficiently!' He was answered by a groan from Lothar. To his horror, the lad sank at his feet in a swoon, staining the straw with his blood. Tristram discovered that the soldier's sword had in fact penetrated Lothar's thigh, yet the brave boy had not uttered the slightest cry of pain, for fear of betraying his friends. With the help of the innkeeper, they lifted Lothar on to Tristram's horse, where he lay half-fainting against the knight's broad shoulder. Iseult mounted another fresh horse and the three set off for the coast. Fortune favoured them: and they managed to elude attention until they reached the lonely cove where Tristram had disembarked.

The Cornish ship lay at anchor! Visions of freedom arose in Iseult's mind, and she began to weep for joy and relief. All their perils seemed to be over, and it was a carefree party who sailed out of the cove on to the high seas towards Cornwall. But they had not been out to sea more than twenty-four hours before one of the sailors reported serious news: a fleet of white sails had been sighted on the horizon, heading towards them at speed.

The Moors had not abandoned the chase so easily! Famed for their seamanship, these dreaded pirates would throw their prisoners into the sea as food for the fishes. Iseult abandoned hope once more and went below to tend Lothar, whose wound was making him restless and feverish. She kept the news of the Moorish sails from him, thinking it of little use to alarm the wounded boy when he could do nothing to stave off their capture. Meanwhile, Tristram and the captain conferred together, and decided unanimously to run for it, and at least give the Moors as much trouble as possible before falling into their cruel hands.

The breeze behind them was strong, and Tristram allowed himself to hope it would carry them out of reach of the Moors before their enemies drew near enough to board them. But little by little the leading Moorish ship gained on them; by the time the coast of Spain had faded away behind them, scarcely a league stretched between them and their foremost pursuer, although the rest of the fleet was some distance behind.

Then Tristram persuaded the sea-captain to take a desperate course. Instead of putting out all his canvas in a hopeless effort to outdistance the faster ship, the captain drew in his sails, which reduced his speed until the two ships were alongside. Momentarily their ship took the wind from the Moorish sails, and while the Moorish canvas flapped idly, Tristram sprang aboard the Moorish ship, brandishing a cutlass, and encouraging the Cornish mariners to follow him. Their onslaught took the Moors completely by surprise, who were busy attending to their own canvas. As Tristram bore down the Moorish captain, only a few brave Moors dared to board the Christian ship as a counter-measure. With his cutlass Tristram was able to slash their rigging and rend their canvas, before ordering his men back on to their own ship.

As he leapt back aboard, he was in time to see the brave sea-captain defending his own rigging with his life against three Moorish sailors. Tristram sprang to his assistance and engaged two of the Moors single-handed, while another Christian attacked the third. Alas, it was too late to save the captain, although the ship itself was still undamaged. He sank to the deck in a pool of blood, just as the Moors were driven off and forced to jump overboard, where they swam rapidly back to their own useless ship. They buried the captain at sea, a sad and solemn ceremony. Then Sir Tristram was left in command of the ship, to bring her back safely to Cornwall.

This was not an easy task, for although the leading Moorish ship was useless, the other ships still snapped at their heels, and their white sails could be seen fluttering ominously in the ocean wind, not nearly far enough away to be comfortable. Tristram blessed the captain for the patience with which he had taught him seamanship.

All this time he had not allowed himself to consider

what would happen to himself and Iseult when they arrived, because it had not seemed worth planning for a future which might never take place. Now, as the days passed, and the prevailing winds blew them relentlessly on to Cornwall, constraint grew up between the knight and his lady. The pursuit of the Moors grew listless, and one fine day the sails turned off towards the coast of France.

Both knew where their duty lay – for Iseult it lay in Cornwall with King Mark; for Sir Tristram with King Arthur and the Knights of the Round Table. Yet both longed for the other to make some move to prevent this sad separation. Many long nights on the deck, watching the stars, Iseult would pray for Tristram to speak to her of his love; while looking out to sea, the knight would wonder if Iseult still loved him. At length the sailors brought the ship safely into the Cornish port. Many were the glances of surprise and curiosity at this strange sight – a lady in Moorish clothes, and a knight in Moorish armour, yet both speaking Cornish and apparently perfectly familiar with the town. Slowly Sir Tristram and the queen made their way to the royal castle, with Lothar dragging behind them, reluctant to disturb their last hours together, for Iseult had confided their terrible situation to him. Sir Tristram was surprised to see that the town was no longer flourishing as if no one cared for its prosperity any longer. He could not believe that King Mark's finances had really taken so long to recover from the Moorish raid. His amazement was completed when he reached the royal castle itself, and found the gates unguarded, the battlements partially ruined, and grass beginning to grow between the pavings of the courtyard.

'Where is the King of Cornwall?' he demanded of a squire.

'Cornwall has no king,' replied the lad rudely. 'It has an overlord at Camelot and that is all.' Sir Tristram drew from him the strange story. Apparently, King Mark, miserly to the last, had refused to acknowledge Arthur's overlordship in spite of his promise to Tristram. He had imprisoned messengers from the Round Table and sent defiant replies to the king. Finally Arthur Pendragon's patience had been exhausted, and he had sent the flower of his chivalry, unmatched in Europe, who made short work of Mark's untrained, ill-armed and seditious army. In a short battle Mark himself had been killed, and his knights made prisoners. The land now lay under the dominion of King Arthur, who was about to choose a suitable governor for it among his own knights.

Sir Tristram and the queen set out at once joyfully for Camelot. Lothar followed them, to seek his fortune at the Round Table. At their entrance King Arthur's own eyes filled with happy tears, as he greeted his knight, and acknowledged the obeisance of Iseult.

'Rise, oh queen,' he cried, 'for you have no need to kneel to me. Since the death of your husband, you are the rightful ruler of Cornwall, of which I am but the overlord. However' – and King Arthur smiled teasingly – 'I advise you to choose a noble knight to help you in your task. How about Sir Lancelot? or Sir Gawaine? or Sir Kay?' Iseult smiled modestly and placed her hand in Sir Tristram's.

'My liege,' she replied in a low clear voice, 'I thank you for restoring to me the kingdom of Cornwall. But of all your knights there is one who I wish to have to help rule my realm, and him I would have as a husband.' Tristram bowed low to his lady, and thanked her for the honour she did him. Their marriage was celebrated in Cornwall with pomp and rejoicing: Lothar was made the first knight in their kingdom, as a reward for his fidelity. Many long years Tristram and Iseult reigned over Cornwall together, in perfect friendship with their overlord, King Arthur.

9

GARETH WINS
HIS SPURS

'Make way for his highness! Way for the great chieftain! Bow before his majesty!' The shouts of laughter and sarcastic offers of homage from the bottom of the hall attracted the attention of the king as he sat at dinner. The squires were sweeping low exaggerated bows, and pretending to kiss the hem of a robe, as if the most honoured guest in the world had come to Camelot. Arthur peered forward. It was indeed an extraordinary and laughable sight which he saw. A boy, for he was no more than that, had ridden right into the hall on the most broken-down, the lamest, the most ill-kempt-looking pony which could have been found in the whole of Britain. Not only that – the youth was dressed in such old-fashioned armour that he looked a figure of fun. His sword was rusty and antiquated. His helmet was far too big. A clumsy lance was strapped to his home-made saddle by rope. To crown it all, his shield was four sizes too small, in contrast to the helmet, and looked more like a toy than a weapon.

But in the midst of all the commotion the boy kept his head and made his way slowly towards the king. When he was forced to dismount his ridiculous horse, he continued to push through the crowd of mocking soldiers until he stood before Arthur himself. The king was amused by his presumption and his lack of fear.

'Well, young fellow,' he said gently, 'you have come before us in curious clothes, but we shall not condemn you for that. All men are welcome at my court, provided they prove themselves to be worthy of the Round Table.'

The king's courteous words stopped the mockery of the soldiers. They saw that Arthur was in one of his lenient moods.

'I crave a boon,' said the young man boldly. King Arthur liked his brashness and laughed out loud.

'Why should I grant you a boon?' he demanded. 'What have you done for me?'

The young man replied that he had done nothing as yet, but he was prepared to serve the king faithfully for a year, if he was granted a boon at the end of it. King Arthur signed to Kay, the Steward of the Household, to draw near.

'I have a new scullion for you, Sir Kay,' he said. 'Give him the lowest tasks in the kitchen to see if he is worthy of being granted his wish.' Sir Kay looked his charge up and down with open contempt. As the young man turned to go, he asked one more question of Arthur:

'Tell me, oh king, which is Sir Gawaine?' King Arthur pointed out the famous knight, who was feasting with Mordred and Balin. The young man stared at him with great interest, and said no more. He followed Sir Kay into the kitchens.

'What is your name, scullion?' asked Sir Kay belligerently when they were out of earshot of the court.

'I am called Gareth,' replied the stranger politely.

'A very ambitious name for such a lowly fellow! I shall

call you "Beaumains" while you are under my orders, for your hands are as white and as smooth as a lady's. I fear you will soil them doing the rough work of the kitchen, but we cannot make allowance for such elegant kitchen boys.'

Gareth continued to smile pleasantly at Kay's spiteful remarks. Nothing Kay said then or at any other time roused Gareth to a temper: he seemed to be impervious to humiliation and suffering. He cooked and roasted meat on the spit, and scoured the kitchen pots and pans with the best will in the world. He allowed the court to call him 'Beaumains' and never objected to their mockery. Gradually his good nature won the affection of his fellow-scullions, and although Kay continued to treat him with scorn, the other knights liked him.

Twelve months from the day Gareth arrived, he was serving the royal banquet in the hall, listening to the demands of the petitioners who were seeking redress at Arthur's court. As Gareth listened to the various appeals, with his mind half on the food he was serving and half on the tales of magic and mystery which were being unfolded, a commotion at the far end of the hall attracted his attention. A beautiful grl, richly clad and adorned with flashing jewels, was seen making her way through the crowd of petitioners. When she reached the royal dais, she made a low obeisance before Arthur and begged him, in the name of the Round Table, to hear her story.

'No one who invokes the name of the Round Table goes away unrewarded,' replied the king gravely. 'Speak, lady, that we may help you in your distress.'

'My name is Linnet,' said the damsel proudly; 'you have probably heard of me for I am famous for my beauty and high birth. I have come to demand your help for my sister Lyonesse, who is besieged in her castle by the Knight of the Red Lands. The knight has besieged her for so long, that she has scarcely any food or water left within the castle, as the knight has terrorized the surrounding farmers, and poisoned the well which is her water supply. Arthur Pendragon, noblest of the British kings, it is your duty to send one of your knights to free my sister.' The boastfulness of the lady Linnet antagonized King Arthur, but he was bound by his oath to listen to any tale of distress. He looked round at Sir Lancelot and Sir Gawaine, his best knights. Sir Lancelot looked carefully in the other direction. Sir Gawaine played with his sword and hummed nonchalantly, as if unconscious of the king's scrutiny. King Arthur looked past them to the younger knights, and found an equal lack of response. The lady Linnet tossed her head and said shrewishly to the king:

'Where is the boasted chivalry of the Round Table? I see that a lady in distress can plead in vain to the knights of Arthur Pendragon.'

Infuriating as her arrogance was, King Arthur was indeed bitterly ashamed of his knights' ill manners. He directed an angry glance at Lancelot, as if to reproach him for his boorish behaviour. Reluctantly, Sir Lancelot put down his goblet, and made as if to rise in answer to the king's mute appeal. At that moment Gareth put down the dish of meat which he had been offering to Sir Bedevere and said in a loud voice:

'Keep your seat, Sir Lancelot. There is one man here who *is* willing to go to the assistance of this lady and her sister. I myself will rescue the lady Lyonesse from the clutches of the Knight of the Red Lands.' To say that the Knights of the Round Table were amazed would be an understatement. They would have been scarcely more surprised if one of the king's own hounds had offered to help Linnet. But Gareth paid not the slightest attention to their laughter. He did not even flinch from the open contempt of the lady Linnet herself. He knelt calmly before the king, and asked him to dispatch him on this mission, as the favour which he had promised him for a year's service.

King Arthur found himself in an acutely embarrassing position; never before had he refused to grant a favour which he had promised to bestow in advance. Never before had he turned away a fair lady in distress from his court. At the same time Gareth could hardly be called a worthy champion for Linnet and Lyonesse. With the greatest reluctance the king nodded his head to Gareth and agreed that he should set forth. He was not surprised to see the disgust on Linnet's beautiful face, which showed what she thought about the king, Gareth, and the whole Round Table. Only Gareth was undismayed by the general consternation. He led the way cheerfully from the hall, with Linnet following haughtily behind him.

Linnet said cuttingly: 'Never in my life have I been used so discourteously. Fancy sending me away with a scullion for a champion! This will make a fine story to tell the enemies of Arthur Pendragon.' Gareth ignored her rudeness and continued to make polite conversation, despite Linnet's brusque replies and sighs of irritation. When night fell she refused to allow him to put up at the same tavern as herself, but forced him to sleep in the hedgerows. She would not permit him to share her food or her wine; Linnet emphasized how disappointed she was at not securing Sir Lancelot or Sir Gawaine to help her.

'You have a sharp tongue in your head, my lady,' remarked Gareth at length. 'Is your sister equally blunt with her champions?'

'You are no champion,' replied Linnet crossly. 'Scullion you are, and scullion you always will be. As for my sister Lyonesse, you will find her every bit as firm with presumptuous scullery boys as I am.'

'In that case,' thought Gareth to himself, 'I do not look forward to meeting the lady, for one of these shrews is enough for any man. The lady Linnet is very beautiful, but I pity her husband, for he will never have a day's peace.' Linnet's pride had been deeply affronted by her reception at Camelot, and she was determined to work off her ill temper on Gareth's innocent head. Gareth's cheerful politeness drove her to distraction, instead of soothing her: for Linnet could only be curbed by firmness; gentleness aroused further spitefulness in her.

Linnet blushed to present Gareth to her sister Lyonesse as the promised champion. Lyonesse looked in open amazement at Gareth's shabby armour and his broken-down horse. Then she noticed Gareth's sturdy build and strong muscular arms. Whatever his birth, at least her champion was no weakling. Whereupon the lady Lyonesse smiled graciously upon Gareth and gave him her hand to kiss, observing to Linnet that she was truly grateful for so gallant a defender.

Linnet tossed her head and could not resist telling Lyonesse that Gareth had until recently been a scullion in Arthur's kitchen. Lyonesse replied that she was especially grateful to Gareth for leaving his duties for such an unworthy cause. Her politeness won Gareth's heart at once: her beauty seemed to him immeasurably greater than that of the haughty and unbearable Linnet, while her sweet nature shone out in her soft words. He kissed Lyonesse's hand with fervour and assured her that he would fight the Knight of the Red Lands until one or other of them surrendered.

'The sooner the better,' put in Linnet. 'Personally, I think we may as well give up hope if our fortunes are to depend upon scullions, but of course I have never *seen* a scullion fight, and so perhaps I am prejudiced.' Lyonesse, however, continued to charm and flatter Gareth, who fell more and more under her spell every minute. He donned his old armour in high spirits and mounted his horse with the best will in the world. Lyonesse and Linnet watched him go.

'The fool!' burst out Linnet. 'The stubborn fool! He is no match for the Red Knight, yet he *would* accompany me, and wrung a promise out of the king to let him go. Exasperating as he was, I cannot but feel sorry for him facing such a famous knight as our enemy, for he does not stand a chance of winning, and the best he can hope for is a severe wound which will overcome him without killing him.'

'You were harsh to him, Sister,' said Lyonesse reprovingly. 'No man fights the better for feeling the rough edge of a woman's tongue. Soft words accomplish more than sarcasm and taunts.' But Lyonesse's philosophy fell upon deaf ears; Linnet retorted that she liked a man to be a man, and not an inexperienced boy who could not stick up for himself.

There was no time for further debate about Gareth, for the two champions were charging each other before their eyes. Gareth made a grotesque spectacle, in contrast to the knight in his superb red armour, with his horse in red trappings. But what he lacked in polish, he made up for in fire and spirit. It was the Red Knight who had to control his terrified horse from fleeing. To Lyonesse's amazement, Gareth proved himself such a doughty fighter that he was able to worst the Red Knight without much difficulty. The craven oppressor did not stop long enough to receive a thorough beating: he set off at a gallop, spurring his horse to get away. Thus Lyonesse was able to step freely out of her castle, in which she had been immured so long, and thank Gareth for his brave show. Linnet, true to her nature, was deeply impressed by the scullion's prowess. She was all smiles when she greeted him, all praises for his skill and all womanly admiration. Now it was Gareth's turn to address her coldly:

'I will not speak to you with the same harshness which you showed towards me, lady Linnet,' said he in an icy voice, which brought the blood into Linnet's cheeks. 'I will content myself with saying that no true lady would have used me as you did. I am as impervious to your gratitude as I was to your bad manners.' Without another word to Linnet, Gareth turned to Lyonesse and devoted himself to her. In vain Linnet begged Gareth's pardon, and swore that he was the very ideal of a perfect knight. Gareth had no use for her affections, for he was absorbed by the lady Lyonesse. She asked him what favour she might grant him, to show how thankful she was for her deliverance.

'There is one favour which I long to demand from the lady Lyonesse,' replied Gareth, blushing hotly. 'But I know full well she will never grant it.'

'Nay,' answered Lyonesse gently. 'Ask me what you

wish and I will grant it, whatsoever it may be.' Then, in a low voice, Gareth told her how much he loved her, and longed to marry her. Now all this time Lyonesse had seen herself in the role of a gracious chatelaine, bestowing a favour upon a good-hearted, but low-born fellow. Thoughts of love and marriage were as far from her mind as they had been from the mind of Linnet before Gareth defeated the Red Knight. But Lyonesse was a great lady, and knew the sanctity of a promise: she could not go back on her word now, no matter what it cost her. Gulping, she said in an equally trembling voice:

'Your request is certainly unexpected, but I have given you my word and I will not break it.' Her goodness aroused Gareth's better feelings: how could he force her into a marriage which it was obvious she would find repugnant? He had behaved unfairly in extracting her promise under false pretences. Controlling himself, he replied lightly:

'Let me change my request, my lady. Come with me instead to the court of the Round Table, for it will give me great pleasure to introduce you to those gallant warriors. Forget that I ever lost my head and asked you to be my bride.'

Lyonesse was immensely grateful to her champion for his courtesy, and despite Gareth's humble station, she felt the first awakenings of real affection for him. She accepted with pleasure his invitation to accompany him back to Camelot, and set off with him the next morning, leaving the disconsolate Linnet to reflect on the value of keeping a civil tongue in her head, and to follow after them at a suitable distance.

Gareth's unfailing politeness did not fail to impress

Lyonesse: as the days passed her heart warmed more and more to this gentle stranger, whose rough clothes were belied by his courteous manners. As their horses climbed the hill to the royal castle at Camelot, Lyonesse took a sudden decision. Laying her hand on Gareth's arm, she said impulsively:

'If you still want to marry me, Gareth, I willingly accept your hand in marriage.' Gareth's joy was plain to see. He dropped his reins and embraced the lady Lyonesse in the sight of the whole court. Radiantly, he led her before King Arthur and explained who she was, and how she had consented to be affianced to him.

'I myself am delighted to knight you, Gareth, for your courage in this affair,' said the king. 'And to welcome the lady Lyonesse to my court. At the Round Table a man's deeds are what matter, and his birth is of little account. In future no one will ever mock you for your lowly birth, Gareth. You have proved yourself to have more than common courage.'

'I thank God that I have won my spurs by my own efforts,' Gareth said. 'Now that I have won them, I can tell you that my birth is as good as any of the Knights of the Round Table. For I am the youngest son of the King of Orkney, and brother to Sir Gawaine.'

His announcement created a sensation at the court. Sir Gawaine leaped from his seat and embraced the brother whom he had not seen since babyhood. King Arthur welcomed the nephew whom he had not recognized. Lyonesse's heart swelled with pride to think that her husband had chosen to make his way in the world without any of the advantages which his royal birth would have given him. Sir Kay had the grace to come forward and apologize handsomely for his former rudeness. Only Linnet could not get over her chagrin at having treated the king's nephew so badly. To think that she might have married him instead of her sister, and been one of the first ladies at court after the queen!

'Scullion you were, and scullion you always will be,' she shouted spitefully, as she flounced out of the court amid roars of laughter from the rest of the knights.

10

GERAINT AND ENID

Geraint of Devon stared round him in dismay. This was not how he had pictured the manor-house of the famous warrior Earl Jocelyn, when he had decided to beg hospitality there on his way to the court of the Round Table. The tapestries were worn and old. The rushes on the floor were old and sparse. The fire was meagre and scarcely warmed the hall. The bedroom into which Earl Jocelyn showed him was both cold and damp. He regretted the impulse which had made him knock on the door of his father's old comrade-at-arms. It would have been better to have ridden on to Camelot. All the excitement at the prospect of winning his spurs was draining out of him at the sight of this decaying house.

Earl Jocelyn made no excuses for his poverty. His arrogant expression defied the young prince of Devon to offer sympathy, or even money for his board and lodging. However, there was one good thing; the house obviously did not lack servants. The rooms were scrupulously clean, if bare, and the food was well cooked. It was handed round by an extremely pretty serving-girl, who impressed Geraint so much by her grace and charm, that he asked Earl Jocelyn who she was after she had left the room.

'She is a servant,' replied the Earl curtly. 'That is all you need to know about her, since it is all that will concern you during your short visit.' Geraint took the broad hint and asked no more questions. But his curiosity was aroused. Late that night, when the Earl had shown him to his room, he gazed out of his window into the courtyard and saw the girl patiently scouring dishes under the pump. After cleaning all her pots and pans, she started to polish Geraint's armour, which the Earl had taken away from him. Geraint had imagined some unseen squire performing this difficult task: at the sight of the girl's struggles, he rushed out of his room and ran down to the courtyard.

'Stop doing that!' he cried imperiously, taking his helmet from her hands. He noticed that although these hands were roughened by hard work, the fingers were long and elegant, as though the girl were of gentle birth in spite of the rough tasks which she performed.

'Let me do it,' replied the girl softly in a charming, low voice that had not a trace of a country accent. 'I am accustomed to polishing armour, and it is no hardship for me.'

'Is there no squire here?' demanded Geraint. 'Where are the Earl's men-at-arms?'

'You see before you the Earl's entire force of serving-women, serving-men, squires and men-at-arms,' she replied, with a hint of a laugh in her voice, as if she found Geraint's questions slightly ridiculous. Geraint was amazed to discover that an Earl who had once been so powerful, should have come down to one girl for his whole establishment. He tried to find out why the Earl had lost all his money, but the girl would not be drawn further.

'Has the Earl no children, to come to his help in his distress?' asked Geraint at length. 'Have I not heard rumours of three beautiful daughters, whose loveliness no less than their rich dowries, brought them many suitors?'

'Misfortune is a great test of character,' replied the girl; her face looked suddenly hard and disillusioned. 'Supposing the Earl's daughters deserted him when he lost his money and his lands, and found husbands in the far-off north of Britain, who could be trusted to ignore the appeals of an ageing and poverty-stricken father?'

'What monstrous behaviour!' exclaimed Geraint indignantly. 'The sort of girl I want to marry when I have won my spurs would stay with her father whatever discomforts she had to put up with.'

A shadow passed over the girl's face, as if his words had touched some chord of sadness in her. Silently, she rose to her feet, gathered up her kitchen vessels and went back into the house. Geraint was left alone to polish his armour and reflect on the beauty and grace of this strange servant-girl. In the morning there was no sign of her. His horse had been well looked after and a hearty meal awaited him in the hall; but the Earl made no attempt to stay him from his departure. Without an excuse to linger, Geraint was obliged to mount and ride off, with the mystery still unsolved.

Geraint Learns the Truth

Nor was it solved for him until many months later, in the course of which King Arthur knighted him, for deeds of daring against King Caradoc. Geraint learned in a casual conversation with Sir Gawaine and Sir Kay, that Earl

Jocelyn had recently died, worn out by poverty and suffering. Geraint took the opportunity to find out why his fortunes had diminished. He learnt that Earl Jocelyn had sacrificed all his money and lands for the sake of his only son, Sir Raynol, who had fallen into debt and appealed to his father to save him from dishonour. Earl Jocelyn had imagined that his beautiful daughters would give up their dowries for this purpose, and at least help the Earl to end his days in comfort, if not luxury. On the contrary, related Sir Kay indignantly, these selfish ladies had wed husbands in the north, and refused to part with a penny to help their father. The Earl's heart had been broken as much by their ingratitude as by his son's debts. When Sir Raynol was killed in a tavern brawl, the Earl remarked grimly that it was as well he had no heir to follow him, since there was nothing left to inherit.

'What a cruel fate,' exclaimed Geraint, 'to have three such ungrateful daughters!'

'Two ungrateful daughters,' Sir Kay corrected him. 'For the third, the lady Enid, was a girl of rare goodness and self-sacrifice. She stayed with her father, gave up her dowry to help her brother, and waited as a servant in her father's house, so that at least he should not have to cook and wash for himself.'

Geraint was electrified by the news that the mysterious serving-girl had been the Earl's own daughter: immediately he decided to ride back to the manor-house and rescue Enid from her distress. But the manor-house proved to be completely deserted when he reached it; and no one could tell him what fate had overtaken the lady Enid. At last one farmer suggested that she had been taken off by Sir Agravaine to his castle in the south. Fired

by love for Enid, Sir Geraint rode all night to Sir
Agravaine's stronghold and hammered on the gates at
dawn. Sir Agravaine himself came out and, recognizing Sir
Geraint as an old opponent in tournaments, offered him
hospitality for the night.

'I have come to seek the hand of the lady Enid in
marriage,' explained Geraint impetuously. 'Show me to
her, that I may offer her my hand and heart together.' Sir
Agravaine scowled, and replied furiously that Geraint
had come on a fool's errand, for his own marriage with the
lady Enid would be celebrated the following morning.
Geraint taunted Sir Agravaine and accused him of forcing
a helpless maid into a marriage which was loathsome to
her; for although he knew nothing of Enid's feelings, he
knew her high ideals of love and unselfishness, and he
could not believe that she was willing to marry a
thoroughly evil knight like Sir Agravaine, with a reputation for cruelty.

The shaft evidently struck home, for Sir Agravaine
swore angrily that he would wed Enid on the morrow
whether she was willing or no, for her reluctance only
made him all the more determined to have his way. He
refused to let Geraint meet Enid. Geraint saw that Sir
Agravaine was on the point of losing his temper, so he
continued to taunt him with remarks about knights who
dared not allow their bride to see any other knight. Sir
Agravaine was unable to endure it a moment longer: he
burst out in a fury:

'Very well, Geraint of Devon, I will put an end to your
taunting once and for all. Let us thrash this matter out
with our swords in the presence of the lady Enid, and if
you master me, you can take the lady to Camelot or not as

you wish.' Sir Agravaine knew perfectly well that he was one of the best swordsmen in Britain, and it was typical of his mean nature that he chose a weapon which suited him, rather than his opponent, without giving Geraint any chance to object. Geraint was too proud to complain – without a word he threw down his glove on the ground and drew his sword. Agravaine ordered Enid to be led out from her chamber and stationed on a small knoll from which she could watch the fight. Enid blushed with happiness to see Geraint again, for she had often wondered what had become of that gallant and good-looking knight who had spoken so kindly to her. She wished that she was not still dressed in the ragged gown in which he had last seen her, the only one she possessed: she wondered if his heart was already given to some beauty at the court of the Round Table.

Little did she know that Geraint was preparing to do battle on her behalf: as she watched the clash of sword against sword, Enid had no inkling that she was the prize which both the knights coveted. She only saw that Geraint fought with passion rather than skill, and that he was hard put to it to hold his own against the experienced Sir Agravaine. It was in fact a cry from Enid which enabled Geraint to slip past his opponent's guard and wound Sir Agravaine. The lady's faint cry of distress caused Agravaine to relax his attention for one fatal moment: it was time enough for Geraint to pierce his mail and fell the knight to the ground. Geraint put his foot on Agravaine's chest and asked him whether he yielded.

'I have no alternative,' replied the knight between gritted teeth. 'But I shall have my revenge one day, Geraint of Devon, on you and your bride.' Geraint dismissed his threats with a laugh, and lifted Enid on to his horse. Together they rode happily back to Camelot, as happy as two lovers can ever be, laughing over the misunderstandings of their last meeting. At Camelot they were wed in front of all the knights, with never a thought of Sir Agravaine.

In spite of her sweet nature, Enid had a strong will of her own. She could not tolerate idleness and self-indulgence – in some ways she was a finer character than Geraint, for her sufferings had made her more mature. Enid was dismayed when the months slipped by at the Round Table and Geraint made no attempt to return to Devon, to look after his vassals and tenants.

THE SUFFERINGS OF ENID

Geraint was the last to notice Enid's distress, and when he did realize that his wife was pining, he jumped to entirely the wrong conclusion about the cause. Like all the knights, he was inclined to be jealous of Lancelot's success with the ladies. No sooner had he decided that Enid had fallen in love with Lancelot, than everything conspired to confirm his suspicion.

One morning Geraint wakened Enid from her sleep and told her to put on the ragged dress in which he had first seen her. Meekly Enid obeyed him, although he refused to answer any of her astonished questions. Then he ordered her to mount an old palfrey, which the merest squire would have disdained to ride, and follow three yards behind him without speaking a word. Enid's amazement grew. Enid decided to accept her new sufferings with the same fortitude which she had shown during the days of her father's poverty. She bore the occasional reproaches which Geraint hurled at her in dignified silence, and tried not to show how deeply he was wounding her. At nights Geraint insisted on putting up at the worst inns where Enid was given particularly unappetizing food, while Geraint himself went out to get a better meal elsewhere. Neither Enid's patience nor her obedience moved his stony heart at all: he put it all down to guilt.

Now their way lay through dangerous country. As they were riding through a narrow defile, Enid noticed four knights spurring towards her husband, from a hidden cutting in the rocks. Geraint had obviously not seen them. It was against human nature to keep silent in these circumstances, and although Geraint had strictly forbidden Enid to speak to him, the lady cried out in dismay:

'My lord! Look out to the right!' Geraint turned round and glared at her. 'Did I or did I not forbid you to address me?' he demanded furiously. 'Be silent, woman, if you do not want to be deserted in the midst of this lonely place.' So saying, Geraint turned his head back, and rode on without looking to left or to right. Thus it was that the four horsemen, armed head to foot, took the proud champion completely by surprise. In vain Geraint hewed at them and stabbed them with his sword; the odds were heavily against him, due to his obdurinacy, and he had no time to choose the most favourable ground to meet the attack. In a short time, Geraint was overcome and bound hand and foot by cruelly tight bonds. Enid's hands were tied behind her back and her horse was led along by one of the knights. She saw no chance of escaping and she was terribly concerned for the fate of her husband.

There was something ominously familiar, too, about the crest which these knights bore upon their shields.

When Enid's captors led her up to a formidable stronghold, with the gate heavily guarded, her suspicions were
confirmed: this was the castle of Sir Agravaine. Even
supposing Geraint survived the clutches of his mortal
enemy, would his love for her ever return? There was no
time to pursue this gloomy train of thought, for Sir
Agravaine himself strode out to meet his victorious
knights. He grinned evilly at the sight of the helpless
Geraint, unconscious from his many wounds. Then he
bowed low to Enid and thanked her sarcastically for the
honour she did him in accepting the hospitality of his
humble castle. Enid said nothing, and ignored his
attempts to help her from her horse. With her head held
high, she walked alone into the great hall where she had
spent so many weary hours of captivity before her
marriage, resisting the obnoxious advances of Sir
Agravaine.

Geraint's senseless body was dumped in a corner. One
of the knights felt his heart and remarked callously:

'The fellow is either dead or dying.' Enid screamed in
spite of herself, and tried to run to his side to attend to him;
but Agravaine held her back, and and told her that the
sooner she forgot Geraint, the better for her. He reminded
her that she was now completely in his power, with no
champion to rescue her, no friends, no weapons of any
sort; and he suggested smoothly that she might like to
devote her attentions to him in future, instead of worrying
herself over a corpse. Enid gazed at him in mute horror;
the thought of life with Agravaine was so utterly distasteful to her, that she would have ridden in silence behind Sir
Geraint for the rest of her life, rather than live in the
utmost luxury with her present captor; disdainfully she

refused all the food and drink which he pressed upon her, although the day had been long and Geraint had allowed her no refreshment.

Agravaine's patience wore thin, and he attempted to force the wine down Enid's throat. The lady screamed loudly at his approach and she cried out desperately:

'As long as I live I shall be true to my lord Geraint, whether I be his wife or his widow!' Her anguished words, and her piercing scream, penetrated the mists of unconsciousness which shrouded Geraint, and aroused him from his stupor. The knights had loosed him from his bonds, thinking him at death's door, and his sword lay to hand. With a mighty effort, Geraint rose to his feet and flung himself upon Agravaine, completely taking the knight by surprise. The attack succeeded by its very rashness – against five knights, Geraint managed to hold his own, and distribute blows which crippled his opponents. Two knights fell to the ground, mortally wounded; then a third; then a fourth; finally only Agravaine himself remained. Geraint summoned all his failing strength and pierced the evil man through and through, before falling back into Enid's arms in another dead faint. When he came to his senses, he was lying on the grass of the forest, with his head in Enid's lap, while his lady bathed his wounds in the water of the nearby stream. Brave Enid had managed to drag her husband out of the dreaded fortress and escape with him to this secluded spot, where she could nurse him in peace. Mutely Geraint pressed her hand, as if to beg her pardon for all the wrong he had done her. Enid said nothing, but smiled gently down at him with such tenderness that he wondered how he could ever have doubted her affection.

When Geraint recovered a little, all their misunderstandings were cleared up. Enid explained her sorrow at
his neglect of his country which had made her pine away
at court, and Geraint confessed with shame his dreadful
suspicions about Sir Lancelot. They swore never to doubt
each other again.

So they set out again for Devon, for a new life after their
ordeals. Geraint resumed the reins of government and
ruled so well that his realm was soon second only to
Cornwall in prosperity. But although he often visited his
old comrades at the Round Table, it needed no hint from
Enid for Geraint to return to Devon. He had learnt his
lesson.

11

SIR GALAHAD AND THE
HOLY GRAIL

'Will the Seat Perilous always be empty?' It was Lancelot who put the wistful question to Merlin. Many times he had glanced enviously at the seat where no one could sit unless he was the best knight in all the world. He often hinted to Merlin that it was time for the seat to be filled, and perhaps he, Lancelot, had the best right to it at the court of the Round Table. But Merlin pretended not to understand him.

'Wait and see, Sir Lancelot,' he would say. 'There will be no doubt when the time comes.' Today Lancelot was more than usually obstinate. He badgered Merlin with questions about the Seat Perilous until the wizard burst out:

'I tell you, Lancelot, that the sin of Elaine is still upon your soul. You shall not occupy that seat.' Sir Lancelot shrank back from his plain speaking. He had hoped that the many services he had done to the poor and weak had absolved him.

'Is there no way I can rid myself of this stain on my honour? Must I endure it until the end of my life?' he asked the wizard humbly. Merlin considered for a moment.

'Yes,' he said slowly, 'there is a way, Lancelot, and I think you are brave enough to take it. Ride out into the forest today and see what you will see.' Greatly puzzled, Sir Lancelot saddled his horse and rode out as the wizard had instructed. He had no idea where he was supposed to go. He let his reins lie slack on the horse's neck, and allowed the animal to guide him. All at once the horse pricked up its ears and quickened its pace. It had been dark in the forest beneath the heavy branches, but now a strange golden light was glimmering through the trees. It grew stronger and stronger until all at once the horse stumbled into a glade which was flooded with such dazzling light that the knight had to shade his eyes. When he opened them again, he started back in surprise: floating among the dark shadows of the trees was the source of all this golden light – a brilliant cloud of brightness, on which rested a gleaming chalice.

Sir Lancelot flung himself on his knees before this holy vision. As he knelt there, uttering fervent prayers, the vision faded and he was left in utter darkness. How many hours Lancelot continued to kneel there in prayer, it is hard to say. A long time later he was conscious of another presence beside him in the forest. It was Merlin.

'Well, Sir Lancelot, did you recognize that vision for what it was – the Holy Grail itself?' asked the wizard. 'The Holy Grail!' exclaimed the knight. 'You mean the wonderful chalice which was used at the Last Supper – the chalice which the infidels captured in the Holy Land and which has been lost to Christendom for hundreds of years! Why, I surely have seen the most marvellous sight in the world.'

'No, there is a more marvellous sight still,' replied

Merlin, 'and that is the Holy Grail itself. Three Christian knights must rescue it from the hands of the enemies of Christ. Will you set out on this perilous quest, Sir Lancelot?'

'I would do anything to set eyes on the Holy Grail itself. I would brave every danger to rescue it.'

'Perhaps you yourself will never set eyes on it,' said the wizard enigmatically, 'although it is written that your flesh and blood shall see it. Are you prepared to take the risk, Lancelot?'

'Willingly I take it. For how can my flesh and blood set eyes upon it, if I do not? I have no kinsman or son who shares my blood I am prepared to take the risk, Merlin.'

'Very well,' said the wizard. 'You have chosen. It shall be so. Follow me now to a neighbouring convent where you may rest and refresh yourself after your experience.'

At the convent Lancelot fell immediately into a deep and dreamless sleep. When he awoke there was no sign of Merlin, but he was surrounded by the nuns, who crowded round him in a great state of agitation. Eventually the abbess herself plucked up her courage and asked Lancelot if he would take an orphan boy who was in their charge to the court of King Arthur. She brought before Lancelot a golden-haired youth, manly and handsome, and already bearing himself like a knight. Lancelot immediately liked the boy, who met his gaze frankly as if he had nothing to fear. He had expected the abbess to produce an effeminate boy used to spending his time among women and therefore reluctant to join in manly sports. But Lancelot discovered that Galahad, as the boy was called, could ride as well as any belted knight, hunt tirelessly all day, and at the end of it still draw a bow with energy and skill.

Lancelot passed happy hours teaching the boy to joust in the convent grounds, until he judged him fit to introduce to Arthur's court. Then he told Galahad to take his farewell of the abbess and the sisters for the time had come for him to seek his fortune in the world.

Lancelot found that Galahad was not only skilled in all the knightly sports: his mind was quick and he took a lively interest in everything which went on around him. Galahad could also argue with ingenuity and hold his own against Lancelot in many a deep discussion. By the time Lancelot reached Camelot he was convinced that Galahad was a rare character and was more than a little curious about his parentage. The only thing that Galahad could tell him was that his mother had died of a broken heart after her husband had deserted her, and that the nuns had taken him as a baby. But he knew neither his mother's name nor his father's lineage. In his own mind, Sir Lancelot was convinced that he must be the son of a knight at least, and no common knight at that.

The Seat Perilous

Proudly he introduced Galahad into the great hall, and pointed out the famous Round Table to him. He told Galahad to find himself a seat among the other squires who were seeking their spurs. To his consternation Galahad paid not the slightest attention but walked boldly up to the Seat Perilous itself, and sat down in it!

No equal sensation had taken place at Camelot since Arthur first drew the sword from the stone and was acclaimed as king. Arthur started from his seat, dropping his goblet from his shaking fingers. The queen turned pale with apprehension and fell back among her women. Lancelot ran forward as if to try to ward off divine wrath from the presumptuous boy. In all this commotion Galahad alone remained unmoved. He sat motionless in the famous seat, his eyes closed, his fair face rapt in some private vision of his own.

'Lo, the prophecy has been fulfilled!' said a deep voice at the king's elbow. Merlin had made one of his silent appearances, and his calm authority restored order to the panic-stricken court.

'This is a blessed sight indeed,' continued the wizard, 'to see the best knight in all the world sitting in the place which was ordained for him since the founding of the Round Table.' The wizard's speech restored Arthur to his senses. He inclined his head graciously to Galahad, as if to signify his approval of the boy, and bade the rest of his courtiers be seated and resume the interrupted banquet. Only Lancelot continued to stare musingly at his protégé, and wonder if this golden-haired boy could be in some mysterious way his own flesh and blood. Towards the end of the evening, Lancelot roused himself from his trance, and stepped forward before the king.

'Harken to me, my liege,' he cried, 'for what I have to say concerns you, no less than all the other knights at this court. For many years I have longed to atone for the many sins which I have committed. Now I think I see the task which God has appointed for me. This very night will I set out to seek the sacred chalice which is called the Holy Grail, and try to rescue it from the hands of the unworthy infidels who guard it. It will be a perilous adventure, but I swear it will be the finest of my generation!' Scarcely had Lancelot finished speaking when many other knights rose to their feet and clamoured to seek the Holy Grail with him. But Merlin urged them all to keep their seats.

'Three knights only shall seek the Holy Grail,' he said. 'Lancelot is one. Who shall the other two be? Who are the two best knights among you, for only he who is without sin shall gaze upon its mystery.' There was little doubt who should be chosen for this honour. Galahad was the obvious first choice – for was he not the best knight in all the world? For the other place, Sir Percival was an outstanding candidate. Sir Gawaine, great knight as he was, was marred by his ambition; Sir Mordred could not altogether conceal the evil depths in his nature from his companions; Sir Kay suffered from a hot temper; Sir Bedevere from covetousness; and so on. Only Sir Percival was universally praised for his goodness of heart. He was chosen by Merlin to stand beside Lancelot and Galahad.

'God be with you,' said the king solemnly. 'With all my heart I envy you in your noble quest. For centuries the Holy Grail has been lost to Christianity and it will take all the resource of three champions to rescue it from pagan hands. But, as Lancelot says, no greater task could be imagined for a knight of the Round Table. God be with you, Lancelot. Percival and Galahad, until we meet again.' With the king's blessing the three knights strode forth from the hall, dedicated to the rescue of the Holy Grail from the hands of the enemies of Christ. One last long look Lancelot exchanged with Queen Gwenevere, to assure her that while he lived, he would always be true to her.

The Quest for the Holy Grail

It was many years since reports of the whereabouts of the Holy Grail had been received in Britain. Rumour had it that the Grail had been immured by the infidels in some stronghold in the depths of the far-off city of Sarras. But even Merlin, with all his spells, could give the three knights no more definite news than this. Only a strong sense of purpose supported the three as they embarked for the east and the Holy Land: but for their faith their mission would have seemed doomed to failure from the very moment of its start. Faith and courage upheld them throughout all their wanderings, all the perils of the long journey to the Holy Land, and all the terrible obstacles which they encountered. It was one year from the day they left Camelot, that the three knights eventually found themselves outside the walls of the city of Sarras. The long journey had left its mark on Lancelot and Percival, but Galahad seemed as fresh and hopeful as he had on the first day Lancelot saw him. Lancelot began to see that Galahad's shining goodness was a source of strength to him in tribulation, when other knights flagged and would have given up. Throughout all their dangers it was Galahad's enthusiasm which inspired them, and prevented them abandoning their search.

Clothed in the humble garb of a pilgrim, with a red cross embroidered on his white cloak, Lancelot gazed at the walls of the city of Sarras, and prayed that he might not be disappointed of the sight of the Holy Grail at this last moment, after he had travelled so far and endured so much in its cause. Percival, too, prayed that he might be rewarded for his sufferings by a sight of the Holy Grail.

Only Galahad had no thought for himself in his prayers, but simply asked God that he might be worthy to rescue the Holy Grail from the hands of His enemies.

It was easy for three humble pilgrims to effect an entrance into the city, for the infidels allowed pilgrims to visit the holy places, provided they came without arms; but it was less easy to discover the hiding place of the Holy Grail. This closely guarded secret could not be discovered by casual inquiry in hostelries, or bribes to infidel soldiers. Lancelot and Percival had almost given up hope, when Galahad awakened one morning from a deep slumber and told them that he had dreamed that the Holy Grail was hidden in a ruined fort some way outside the city of Sarras. All Lancelot's doubts could not shake Galahad from his conviction that the dream was a vision sent by God to guide them. He insisted on setting out at once for the ruined fort. The tumbledown walls, rising out of the lonely sands, did not inspire confidence. Impossible to believe that the Holy Grail itself was concealed here! Yet a hundred times on their journey it had been proved that God looked with special favour upon Galahad and revealed things to him in dreams which ordinary mortals were not permitted to know. Lancelot recalled that the infidels were as cunning as the devil himself: the deserted appearance of this place would certainly put off all but the most determined seekers.

Galahad went forward first and scouted round the ruins. He had just set foot within the second courtyard when a muscular brown arm shot out from behind a pillar, caught him round the neck and bore him to the ground. His strangled cry warned Lancelot and Percival. They rushed to his assistance. Half a dozen of the infidels tried to beat them off, but three Christian knights were enough to defeat a score of unbelievers. In that fight alone Lancelot would have won himself a reputation for valour which many other knights never achieved in a lifetime. As for Percival, he flung himself into the fray with whirling sword and plunging dagger. It was Percival who shed the first blood on the sands. Immediately Galahad started back in horror and begged him to stay his hand.

'Shed no more blood in this holy place, Percival,' he implored him. 'Bind the infidel hand and foot, but do not desecrate the home of the Holy Grail with bloodshed.' Deeply ashamed of his rashness, Percival begged Galahad's pardon, and contented himself with tying up their adversaries securely. Then they herded the guards into a back room, and locked the door upon them. One of the keys from the belt of the leading guard attracted Lancelot's attention by its intricate workmanship, which distinguished it from the rest of the bunch. Taking this key, he tried it in several locks, until it finally fitted smoothly into the lock of a great studded door in the centre of the fortress. Within the walls, the stronghold was in excellent repair, and great trouble had evidently been taken to make the defences secure, while preserving the ruined appearance of the place from the outside. Beckoning to Galahad and Percival, Lancelot stepped warily through the unlocked door, and found himself in the deepest darkness. All three tumbled heavily down a flight of stone steps, and landed in a heap at the bottom, without being able to distinguish a thing. When their eyes grew more accustomed to the darkness, they managed to make out the vaulted roof of a great underground room about their heads, and vast buttressed walls around them. Did some dim light shine forth from the far end of this subterranean chamber? The brightness seemed to grow stronger every minute, filling the dark room with a soft, golden light. Lancelot was instantly reminded of his vision in the forest. In a moment he realized that the Holy Grail itself lay near to them, to cast its legendary lustre upon them. The three champions fell on their knees in prayer. It was Galahad who was the first to rise up and move slowly towards the glowing light. But when Lancelot and Percival would have followed him, invisible hands seemed to hold them back, and root them to their knees upon the stone floor. Lancelot and Percival found they could not move hand or foot. Powerless to protest, they watched Galahad pass like a spirit through the now dazzling cloud of light at the end of the chamber. One moment his fair head was illuminated as if by a halo. The next moment all the light had faded, and the two knights knelt alone, desolate and motionless in the dank subterranean darkness.

Sir Galahad Vanishes

They knew not how long they knelt thus, before a deep familiar voice at their elbow startled them. Merlin himself stood there, gazing steadily at Lancelot, a gaze in which sympathy and sorrow were mixed. The knight found that the spell had now broken, and he could move freely. He leapt to his feet, and with Percival hard on his heels would have broken down the mysterious door at the end of the room, through which Galahad had been seen to pass. Merlin restrained them with a word.

'Too late, Sir Lancelot,' he said sadly. 'The Holy Grail

has been taken up into heaven, with its faithful knight Sir Galahad to guard it. Many a time I warned you that only he who was without sin amongst you should gaze upon its mystery. With all your nobility, Lancelot, you were not worthy to see the Holy Grail itself, and as for you, Percival, the finest of Arthur's knights, did you not wilfully shed blood, here in the fortress of the Holy Grail itself?' Then the full realization of what they had lost smote the two knights, and they wept bitterly for the sins which had prevented them from gazing upon the most wondrous sight in the world – the Holy Grail. Lancelot's grief was the more bitter – for not only had he lost the Holy Grail, he had also lost Galahad, who was dearer to him than any other knight in the world. The great champion's heart felt as if it would break, when he reflected that never again would he joust with the boy, or talk with him, or sit with him in silence, quietly rejoicing in the comfort of his company. Merlin read Lancelot's thoughts. He put his hand on the knight's shoulder.

'Did I not prophesy that your flesh and blood should gaze upon the Holy Grail?' he said solemnly. 'Then learn, Lancelot, that Galahad was no other than your own son, the son of Elaine of Astolat, whose tragic death stained your honour and kept you from the presence of the Holy Grail.'

'My son!' cried Lancelot, in a tumult of emotion, grief for what he had lost, astonishment at this revelation, and joy that the beloved Galahad should in fact have been his own son. 'Blessed be God for this piece of comfort in my agony. No longer shall I mourn for what I have lost, but I shall rejoice all the rest of my life that Galahad, the best knight in all the world, was my own son.' Merlin explained that Elaine had given birth to Galahad a short while before her death, and had consigned the child to the convent where Lancelot first met Galahad, with instructions that the boy was to be dispatched to the Round Table on his eighteenth birthday. She had sworn the abbess to secrecy about the child's lineage, and but for Merlin's magic knowledge, the secret might have remained locked in the abbess's heart for ever.

Then Lancelot drew apart from Percival and Merlin a little, to ponder on the mysterious ways of God, who had rewarded his cruel treatment of Elaine by giving him a peerless son. When his sorrow had abated a little, and tender memories of Galahad flooded back to console him, he returned to Merlin and vowed that he would spent the rest of his life in the service of the right, that he might be judged worthy to join Galahad in heaven at his death. With the wizard's approval, Lancelot and Percival left the lonely fortress, and began the long journey back to Camelot. When they finally reached the court, after wandering half round the world, seeing many strange sights and experiencing many curious adventures, there was not one knight who failed to mark the change in them. Marks of suffering furrowed Lancelot's handsome face, and he had the air of a man who had undergone so much tribulation that his nature had been purged of all worldly thoughts. Gwenevere noticed that, although Lancelot paid her all the courtesies which were her due, as the lady he had sworn to serve, there was more respect and devotion than ardent love in his manner. Lancelot seemed at last to have conquered his passionate nature, which had been the cause of his undoing with Elaine. In the years which remained to him, Lancelot was never seen to speak an unkind word, or do an unworthy deed. The quest of the Holy Grail, however poignant and unsuccessful, had given him an ideal to live up to. Percival, too, had been purified by the quest: for he gave up his life to the troubles of others, giving no thought to his own advancement.

Thus the Holy Grail, the wonderful sight which no man could see unless he was without sin, had stretched forth its unseen influence over the two knights who remained on earth. Galahad looked down from heaven and rejoiced that the quest had not been in vain.

12

KING ARTHUR AT
THE CASTLE PERILOUS

*K*ing Arthur examined his beard sadly. Were these silver hairs the sign that all his adventures were over? It was now many years since the founding of the Round Table. Arthur decided to have one more adventure before old age claimed him. Without saying a word to anyone – which showed that he had a slight feeling of guilt about the whole affair – he crept out of the castle one early summer's morning, armed only with Excalibur, and clothed in a plain suit of armour which did not bear the unmistakable royal arms. King Arthur felt like a schoolboy playing truant. With his visor down, he slipped past the guard as just another wandering knight who had claimed royal hospitality for the night. Never had Arthur's spirits been higher, even in the first flush of youth when he accepted the cares of kingship in a joyous spirit of adventure.

Yet he had no plans for the future, and no idea where to seek adventure. Life seemed too good to spoil it with worry. Arthur felt sure that some escapade would come his way before the day was out. If Arthur had looked behind him, he might not have felt so blithely confident that the adventure would be such a lighthearted affair. Arthur's furtive exit had not been altogether unobserved after all. Tossing restessly on his couch, with the uneasy sleep of those who are gnawed by discontent and ambition, Mordred had been awakened by the clop-clop of Arthur's horse's hoofs on the cobbles. Mordred had not watched every movement of the king with fierce jealousy for nothing. There was not an action of Arthur's which Mordred was not convinced he could perform better if he were king. Unknown to all at court, Mordred had been seeing his mother, Morgan Le Fay, in secret, and listening to the poisoned words which she delighted to drop in his ear.

'Ah, you would have been the king, if justice had been done,' Morgan Le Fay would exclaim, shaking her head. 'Was not your father the noblest king in the west in his day? He would have ended his days on the throne if it had not been for the deceitful upstart, Arthur Pendragon, and that pernicious wizard, Merlin. One day I shall have my revenge on both of them.'

'I shall help you, mother,' vowed Mordred, his face flushing at the thought of the injustice which Arthur had done to his father. 'Together let us encompass the destruction of Merlin, and the fall of the king. I have put up with slights too long at this court, and I will not endure it a month longer. Am I not a better fighter than Percival or Gareth? Yet both of these were chosen before me to be the king's champion at the tournament of Epiphany. The queen smiles upon Lancelot, but she treats me coldly although I am a kinsman of her husband.' Morgan Le Fay rejoiced to see that she had planted the seeds of rebellion in Mordred's bitter heart: he had forgotten all the kindness which Arthur had shown him in bringing him from childhood, in knighting him, endowing him with a castle and lands, and giving him a position at court which was greater than he deserved. Mordred's restless nature was never content with what he had got. The apple out of reach was always the most desirable friut on the branch.

Now that Mordred marked a strange knight riding out of the castle, and alone, and remembered that no stranger had spent the evening at the Round Table, his febrile mind searched round for an explanation. Was there not something familiar about the bearing of this knight? Something regal about the tilt of the head in its helmet? With a bound Mordred was off his couch and pulling on his clothes. Morgan Le Fay should hear of this before another hour passed.

All unconscious of the dark plots which were being hatched in a certain lonely castle on the wind-swept moors north of Camelot, Arthur rode on, singing merrily to himself. Night fell, and in the darkness the country seemed unfamiliar, but Arthur had Excalibur by his side and naught to fear. It was while his horse was picking its way through a causeway lined with flinty stones and fallen boulders, that Arthur first spied the spiky turrets of a castle, outlined against the night sky. The wind had risen to a gale, and driving rain lashed both man and horse. The moon was partly hidden by storm-clouds and the castle looked both remote and menacing in the eerie light. The needs of his horse, rather than Arthur's own inclinations, decided him to climb the mountain and seek refuge at this lonely fortress. As he reined in his horse and peered through the darkness for a track up the hill-side, a curious sensation of dampness sent shivers down his spine. He felt his horse's flanks. They were soaking wet, as though with dew, and yet this was clearly impossible for four or five hours. Arthur looked around for a marsh or fountain to explain this phenomenon. In the darkness nothing was visible except rocks, throwing shadows across the road, and occasionally scrubby bushes. Nothing to suggest that the land was particularly well-watered. Then a soft ghostly sigh behind Arthur made him jump nervously: his fear communicated itself to his horse, who reared up and whinnied, pawing with its hoofs in the air. Once Arthur had mastered the frightened animal, he was able to peer closely at the nearest boulder from which the unearthly sound had come. There was definitely something sitting there, something muffled in dark cloaks and veils, something whose face, if it had a face, was so turned that the light of the moon did not strike it.

'Alas!' The single softly spoken word had the effect of chilling Arthur's blood. An absurd impulse to spur his horse to flight seized him. He fought it down; again that curious feeling of dampness pervaded his very bones, and moreover a subtle smell of decay hung upon the air, as though the king were stepping into some long-forgotten dungeon mildewed by the centuries. Like many another brave man before him, Arthur took refuge in bravado to hide his fear.

'Show your face!' he cried, 'and reveal your sorrow, whoever or whatever you be.' Another sigh was his only answer, a sigh so deep and despairing that it seemed to fill the air with sadness.

'Speak, else I will run you through with my sword,' cried Arthur.

'Do not do that,' said the voice softly. 'For however unhappy my lot, I have no wish to die. It was to implore assistance that I seated myself on this rock and waited for some noble knight to come by.' The voice was clearly that of a woman.

'What is your trouble, lady?' asked Arthur cautiously.

'Alas, alas,' wept the unknown. 'My castle, which you see there on high, is beset by a magic knight, who will claim it at dawn tomorrow, if I can find no champion to defend me. Who can fight a magician and win? Tomorrow I shall be homeless.' All Arthur's instincts warned him to distrust this story. But Arthur fingered his greying beard and threw caution to the winds. 'I'll show Lancelot he is not the only person who rescues ladies in distress,' he thought. Recklessly Arthur agreed to accompany the lady up the winding path to the castle.

All this time he had still not had a glimpse of her face, and even when they reached the top of the mountain where the gaunt stone walls of the fortress glowered down on them, the lady was careful to keep her face out of the lamplight. Arthur gazed about him with a certain amount of apprehension. Now that the great gates were closed behind him he began to wonder what he had let himself in for. The lady, speaking from the shadows, offered to take his armour and polish it for him, in readiness for the fight on the morrow. Arthur was reluctant to part with Excalibur, but the lady pointed out one or two spots on the matchless blade which marred its beauty. She promised to remove them with a special ointment. Then she showed Arthur to a richly-hung bed- chamber, with tapestries showing scenes of water lining the stone walls. As the door closed behind his hostess, Arthur felt once more the familiar damp sensation which had made him shudder in the valley. Here, up high among the mountains, it was even more puzzling. Surely no marsh could exist so far above the rivers and plains.

At dawn he stirred and found his armour lying neatly laid out beside him. There was no sign of his hostess but his bedroom door was open. His horse was standing in the courtyard, and the gates of the castle had been opened to let him ride out on to the turf outside. Arthur buckled on his armour and girded himself with his sword. Was it his imagination or did Excalibur seem lighter than usual? Arthur drew out the famous sword and examined it. The lettering on each side of the blade had been well polished. There was no doubt it *was* Excalibur. There could not be two swords engraved with 'Keep me' on one side and 'Cast me away' on the other. But he still fancied it weighed lighter in his hand than usual.

Arthur dismissed the matter from his mind and mounted his horse. He had scarcely taken up his position outside the castle when he espied his opponent galloping towards him. Something about the way the strange knight handled his horse struck Arthur as vaguely familiar. But he had no time to analyse the resemblance. His opponent was coming at him at full tilt. Suddenly the knight reined in his horse and signed to Arthur that he should dismount. He pointed to his sword and indicated that they should fight on foot. Arthur was only too pleased. With Excalibur in his hand he was even more formidable than with his lance. Joyfully he drew the trusty blade and advanced on the Magic Knight.

The first few cuts and thrusts decided nothing either way; but as the fight proceeded, Arthur found to his amazement that Excalibur, so trusty for so many years, was bending beneath the weight of his opponent's blows! Arthur was so unprepared for this disaster that his nerve went, and he began to retreat instinctively from the fray.

The Magic Knight pressed on, thrusting his own sword forward with all his might, and flashing the blade to and fro in the first red rays of the sun. It was in one of these wide sweeps that Arthur noticed the lettering on the sword – the three words 'Cast me away'. In a flash he realized the solution to his own sword's strange weakness: the sword with which his opponent was beating him slowly backwards was none other than Excalibur itself! He himself was holding no more than an imitation in his hand, which was no match for the famous masterpiece of the sword-maker's art.

Arthur had one minute in which to reflect that this was a poor way for a great King to die, at dawn outside a lonely castle, in the hands of a sorcerer, when a blinding flash lit up the sky, and he fell senseless to the ground. The next thing the king knew, he was being shaken gently by the wizard Merlin, who was holding out the sword Excalibur to him. Arthur looked wildly round for any trace of the Magic Knight and saw none; the castle itself seemed to have changed its aspect, for it now looked ruined and deserted, and the gates which had gleamed in the first rays of the sun, now appeared rusty as if they had not been used for a score of years.

'Where am I?' asked the king in bewilderment, holding his head in his hands and clutching his aching brow.

'Do not fear, Arthur,' replied the wizard. 'I have saved you from the consequence of your folly at the Castle Perilous.'

'The Castle Perilous? It is well-named indeed,' said Arthur ruefully. 'For I was likely to have succumbed to its perils, through my own foolishness.'

'Learn that this castle belongs to the queen of the

Waterwitches herself,' went on Merlin. The king started and exclaimed: 'Then that explains the dampness which I felt in the air around her and the strange tapestries all on the same subject! Fool that I am, why did I not guess that some magic was afoot from that unearthly moisture which clung to my hands and face, and even the flanks of my horse!'

'It is easy to be wise after the event,' Merlin could not resist saying. 'Some people might say that the king who rode out of his castle alone in the early morning, with some fool idea of imitating the adventures of his youth, was asking for trouble. Oh, Arthur Pendragon, how could you fall for such a hackneyed tale as the knight who fights at dawn, and the lady in distress whose castle is besieged and needs a champion?'

'That's enough, Merlin,' replied the king, blushing. 'I am not proud of the incident, and I shall rest content with governing my kingdom in future, since my attempts at knight-errantry are so unsuccessful. Do you remember the time when Morgan Le Fay stole my scabbard? Very nearly the same trick, too. The witch-queen doesn't seem to have learned much in twenty years,' Merlin agreed. He revealed to Arthur that the queen of the Waterwitches was an old ally of Morgan Le Fay and had been persuaded to act as the decoy in the trap.

Arthur eagerly demanded who his adversary had been and confided to the wizard that his style of fighting was faintly familiar. Merlin paused impressively. 'That was your kinsman Mordred,' he declared. Arthur stared back at him angrily.

'Mordred, a knight of the Round Table, in league against his king!' cried Arthur. 'It is treachery even to suggest such a thing, Merlin. I myself reared Mordred after the flight of his mother, and taught him all the arts of chivalry myself. Mordred would not think of betraying me, for it would be like betraying his own father.' In vain Merlin told the king that a canker of resentment had eaten away in Mordred's heart for many years, and he had been seeing his evil mother in secret. Even when Merlin swore on his oath as a wizard that Mordred had been seen in conversation with Morgan Le Fay that very morning, by one of Merlin's spies, Arthur still refused to believe him. With anguish in his face, Arthur vowed that he would rather believe that Gwenevere herself was a traitor than one of the Knights of the Round Table had conspired to betray his king.

'Arthur Pendragon,' cried Merlin at last, his patience exhausted. 'There will come a time when you will regret your idiotic obstinacy! Then I hope you will recall the words of the faithful wizard who tried to warn you, and blush for very shame. In the meantime I will leave you to your own devices. Twice already you have been outwitted by Morgan Le Fay, through your folly. A third time I fear you will not get off so lightly.' With these ominous words, the wizard rode off in a huff, promising himself never to utter another word of advice to the stubborn fool who sat upon the throne. He left Arthur equally angry, and swearing in turn to give Merlin no further opportunity to gloat over him. He decided that old age was leaving its mark on the wizard, and that his brain was no longer quick enough to interpret his own magic. That evening at Camelot, Arthur took especial pleasure in showering favours on Mordred, to Merlin's sorrow. Merlin knew that Mordred's smile betokened only evil for the realm.

13

THE DOOM OF MERLIN

King Arthur was not the only person at court who was troubled by the onset of old age. Merlin himself discovered that his magic powers were waning, and that he could no longer weave a spell with the skill of his youth. In vain he practised all his old arts – read the future frantically, turned a veritable mountain of stones into frogs and vice versa, created thunder-storms every other minute, turned the rivers red and so on and so on. He could not conceal from himself that his hand had lost its cunning. He could still read the future up to the next twenty-four hours or so, but the distant future looked increasingly hazy when he examined it.

'Old and out of work, that is how I shall end my days,' thought the wizard gloomily 'Who will have time to spare for a wizard who cannot even create enchantment?' Arthur will turn me out and give the place of honour which has been mine for a thousand years to another younger man.' In his heart of hearts Merlin knew that he did not do Arthur justice, for the king would never have abandoned his faithful friend. But a slight coldness had grown up between the king and the wizard since the incident of the Castle Perilous. Merlin studiously refrained from giving

Arthur advice, and Arthur would have died rather than ask it. The two stubborn men greeted each other politely but distantly when they met, and paid each other elaborate courtesies in public.

Thus when Merlin was seized with his inspiration, he had no friend to warn him against the consequences of his own folly. For so long the wizard had been a figure of awe to the Knights of the Round Table, they could not have imagined that he himself was now in need of the advice which he had often given them. It was while wandering disconsolately in the meadows by the river that Merlin espied an outstandingly beautiful girl walking by herself, with a basket of wild flowers and herbs over her arm. She could not have been more than seventeen or eighteen, and the wizard's heart was won as much by the innocence of her lovely face as by its flawless perfection of feature and colouring, and in a flash the idea came to the wizard that the very thing which would save him from a lonely old age would be a young and charming wife to look after him.

With this idea seething in his mind, Merlin half consciously and half unconsciously began to follow the girl. She appeared not to notice his interest, but continued to walk through the fields in a stately fashion, plucking a flower from here and a herb from there. Suddenly she paused and frowned, and stretched her white arms vainly towards a flower-laden bough above her head. It was out of reach. The maiden bit her pretty lip and gazed round for assistance. This was Merlin's chance. He hobbled forward and, with his skinny fingers, plucked the whole bough from the tree. The girl's amazement was obvious: for how could such a frail old man have torn the bough from the tree with such superlative ease. She curtsied and took the bough from his hand.

'That was a kind deed, good sir,' she said in her soft childish voice. 'For my mistress bade me to be sure to gather some of this blossom, and I could never have reached it by myself.'

'It was nothing,' replied the wizard grandly, waving an expansive arm to indicate that he could get every flower in the kingdom for her if she wanted them. 'What is your name, my pretty one? For I have never seen you at court. As for me, I am called Merlin – a name which you may possibly have heard of,' the wizard could not resist adding proudly. But not a flicker of recognition passed over the girl's lovely face. She stared at Merlin blankly and replied:

'I am not one of the ladies of the court. They call me Vivian, and my mistress dwells to the north of this town. I am here to collect the famous herbs which grow in the water-meadows of Camelot.'

'Not at court!' exclaimed Merlin gallantly. 'That explains why the queen is still thought to be the fairest lady there. If you were there, no knight would look twice at anyone else, I can assure you.' The girl laughed gaily. 'What chance have I of ever coming to court?' she demanded. 'For I have no sponsor who would introduce me there.' Merlin seized his chance.

'You see before you one who would be only too happy to perform that task,' he said, with as graceful a bow as he could manage. Vivian gazed at him, opening her large eyes wide.

'You would do that for me?' she cried. 'Why, I think you are the kindest person in all the world.' The wizard cast his eyes down modestly and replied that anyone would be happy to help such a charming and well-mannered young lady. Vivian agreed to meet him on the same spot the next morning, when she would have taken leave of her mistress and collected her few belongings. Merlin hurried back to the castle and sought an audience of the queen. He told her that he had found her a new waiting-woman of such surpassing beauty that she would set all her husband's knights by the ears. Gwenevere listened calmly to Merlin's enthusiastic praises and remarked acidly that in her experience beautiful waiting-women were more trouble than they were worth. They were either married within the month, or else stirred up so much mischief that they had to be asked to leave the court.

'Vivian is different,' replied Merlin proudly. 'She is good and modest and charming.' Gwenevere answered tartly that the wizard had apparently discovered a lot about this paragon in the course of one short interview in the fields; but when she questioned the wizard about the girl's lineage and background, she found that he had not the slightest idea where she came from. Gwenevere shrugged her shoulders in despair and reflected that old age was making the distinguished wizard foolish. However, great affection had always existed between her and Merlin, and she agreed to take Vivian into her retinue for his sake.

The next day Merlin combed his grey locks with enormous care and put on his best cloak. He chose a polished stick from among his collection, and borrowed a looking-glass from the queen to survey the general effect. Gwenevere could not help smiling to herself to see the pains the wizard was taking to impress this chit of a girl, yet all this time no premonition of the consequences of Vivian's arrival crossed their minds. So dim had Merlin's magic become lately, that the future was hidden from him altogether, at the very time when he had most need of all his arts to ward off the perils which threatened him.

A Spy at the Court

Had he no pang of apprehension at the sight of Vivian standing meekly beneath the apple tree, a grey cloak muffling her long hair, and a small bundle at her feet? It is difficult to believe that Merlin, the greatest wizard in Britain for a thousand years, did not sense the evil magic emanating from the innocent-looking girl.

Only an hour before, Vivian had knelt before her mistress Queen Morgan Le Fay and sworn to use all the arts she had taught her to bring about the destruction of Merlin. As Vivian swore the oath, Morgan Le Fay reflected with delight that at last fate had played into her hands and given her the weapon which would bring about the downfall of Arthur. Without Merlin, Morgan Le Fay would have defeated Arthur long ago. Oh, joyful chance that had brought her favourite pupil Vivian and Merlin together! Had Morgan Le Fay believed in God she would have thanked Him fervently for this coincidence. As it was, she said to herself proudly that the many spells which she had woven for Arthur's destruction must have borne friut at last.

'A million greetings,' cried Merlin now, as he gazed rapturously at Vivian. She seemed even more beautiful than she had the day before. Such a lovely girl would make a fitting bride for an ageing wizard. He would teach her all his magic arts, and in return she would tend him faithfully and preserve him from loneliness. Thus the ill-assorted couple made their way to the castle, causing many rude passers-by to stare and make remarks about winter and spring going hand in hand. Merlin felt he could afford to ignore their ill-bred comments. It was only when he looked at Vivian to see how she was taking them, that his composure was slightly upset. He could have sworn that he caught a malicious smile of triumph on her pretty face. The next moment Vivian was meeting Merlin's inquiring gaze blandly, with a shy smile and a flutter of the eyelashes. Merlin dismissed the malice as imagination.

Merlin's infatuation with Vivian increased from day to day. It became the subject for ribald jokes with the elder knights, who were happily married, and could afford to look down on such goings-on as undignified. Sir Lancelot never encountered the wizard without asking anxiously after his grand-daughter. A dozen times Merlin replied that she was not his grand-daughter, but a young friend; a dozen times Sir Lancelot apologized profusely, and answered that of course Merlin had no grand-daughter – how stupid of him to forget. Gawaine taught Vivian to hunt and hawk, driving the wizard to distraction by occupying Vivian's time all day, and tiring her to such an extent that she only wanted to creep into bed in the evening, and refused to go dancing with her aged protector. Gareth introduced Vivian to his young half-brothers, gallant youths, newly come to the Round Table, who were delighted to be presented with such a pretty girl to entertain. The knights were unkind to the poor wizard, but to do them justice, none of them realized how deeply Merlin's affections were involved with Vivian. They looked on his infatuation as a passing whim, the caprice of an old man, which he could be laughed out of. None of them realized that he intended to wed Vivian in a matter of months, and the wizard had not the moral courage to confide his project to anyone. One day he did pluck up enough courage to ask Gwenevere if she thought marriages between the very young and the very old were impossible.

'Beware of a young wife, Merlin,' replied Gwenevere, laughing. 'She will spend all your savings and deceive you left and right.' But Vivian was not like that, thought the wizard stubbornly to himself. It was lucky for his peace of mind that he could not see Vivian climbing out of her turret at night by a rope-ladder which Morgan Le Fay had given her. This apparently frail girl, so delicate that hunting with Gawaine wore her out, had the strength to climb down the dizzying heights of the castle and scale a ten foot wall. Once outside the castle walls, Vivian's whole demeanour changed. The appealing helplessness which endeared her to Merlin vanished: she became bold and resolute, eager to do Morgan Le Fay's bidding, no matter how evil.

Her nightly progress report to the witch queen took the form of long, gloating chuckles over the wizard's foolishness. Vivian promised that within a month she would have shorn Merlin of his powers for ever.

'Have you no fondness at all for the old fool?' asked Morgan Le Fay curiously, for even she was sometimes taken aback by the contrast between Vivian's soft expression and her cold, calculating heart.

'Fondness?' repeated Vivian contemptuously. 'I have never known what that word means. What is affection?

What is love? Both of them seem to lead people into trouble, and long ago I resolved not to let myself be trapped in the same way.' Half-witch, half-woman as she was, Morgan Le Fay could not help sighing a little in secret at her pupil's utter heartlessness. For Morgan Le Fay was not devoid of all tender feelings: she had loved her husband passionately, and her ambitions were now wrapped up in her son, the younger Mordred. However, if Vivian's callousness was going to lead to the success of her plans, Morgan Le Fay was in no position to complain.

Perhaps she would have been more concerned if she had known that Vivian planned to wed Mordred after the *coup d'état* unseated Arthur from the throne. Vivian had long matured this plan as the easiest way of seizing power, and she was determined to let nothing stand in her way. But Morgan Le Fay had given few thoughts to Vivian's future and assumed carelessly that she would end her days as a waiting-woman.

About a fortnight after this conversation, Vivian met Mordred pacing up and down the cathedral cloisters at Camelot. This quiet, shady place was generally deserted. Mordred often walked there, meditating on his future. Vivian had noticed his fondness for the place, and seized her opportunity. She was aware that as yet Mordred knew nothing of Morgan Le Fay's plan for getting rid of Merlin, and in Mordred's eyes Vivian was just another of the frivolous girls at court. Mordred's first reaction at sighting the girl was disgust that even here one of Gwenevere's waiting-women had followed him, with her silly chatter. When he saw it was the girl whom the wizard Merlin was making a fool of himself about, his irritation increased rather than lessened.

'Good morning, lady,' said Mordred coldly.

'Good morning, my liege,' replied Vivian, dropping a curtsy. The unusual address caught Mordred off his guard, for only the king was usually called 'my liege', and Vivian's words awakened all his seething jealousy.

'Do not call me that,' he answered roughly. 'Are you so country-bred that you do not know that only the king is addressed as "my liege"?'

'Only the rightful king,' replied Vivian significantly. Her eyes met those of Mordred in a long, searching look. Neither spoke. Then Vivian dropped another curtsy and swept out of the cloisters without another word. She left Mordred staring after her in mingled surprise and excitement: for was it possible that there was a core of dissatisfaction with Arthur's rule at Camelot, under the peaceful surface? Was Mordred's hour coming at last?

The next day at the tournament, Mordred fought with especial valour and acquitted himself so well that Arthur awarded him the prize of a wreath of leaves, to put round his helmet. Instead of putting on the wreath, Mordred took it on his lance, and rode over to the queen's pavilion, where Vivian was watching the fighting with the rest of the ladies. Inclining his head to Gwenevere, Mordred asked her permission to bestow the wreath upon Vivian. Gwenevere was only too pleased to give permission. It seemed to her optimistic nature that a match between Mordred and Vivian would solve two problems. Merlin would be cured of his silly infatuation, and Mordred would throw off the solitary ways which worried Arthur.

Again a long, searching look passed between Vivian and Mordred, as the victor extended his lance towards the girl. Each knew that the gift of the wreath stood for something more than the gesture of a gallant knight to a pretty girl. It was the symbol of an unholy alliance. Vivian smiled to herself, well pleased.

Merlin Seals His Fate

But Mordred's public action had driven Merlin to frenzy. He felt that he was going to be robbed of his bride by the devil himself: for Merlin still had enough sense to distrust Mordred's intentions, even if he could not foresee the exact form which his evil actions would take. He could not contemplate the possibility of the fair and innocent Vivian getting involved with blackhearted Mordred. He resolved to ask Vivian to marry him that very evening. He made his way to the queen's pavilion and begged a word with Vivian. She greeted him with her usual docility and at once agreed to walk with him in the forest that evening at sunset when the heat of the day had passed. Vivian could see from Merlin's agitated state, which he could not altogether hide, that the critical moment had come. Immediately she dispatched a messenger to Morgan Le Fay, bearing these cryptic words:

'Tonight at sunset in the forest of Broceliande.' Morgan Le Fay read them in her northern castle, and her thin lips twisted in a diabolical smile.

'Now Merlin, you will see whose magic is more powerful,' she said aloud. 'The hour of reckoning is at hand. Without your help, Arthur Pendragon will not long survive, and then my son Mordred will be king, as his father was before him.'

It was a calm evening that day at Camelot. No winds stirred the thick branches of the forests as Vivian walked with Merlin through the trees. As the last rays of the sun struggled through the leaves and turned the dim forest light in turn gold and pink, Merlin tried to pluck up courage to tell Vivian what was on his mind. But the girl seemed inclined to walk farther and farther into the forest. Whenever Merlin suggested that they should pause and rest awhile, she urged him on, pointing to the next glade and then the next. Merlin's old bones soon became weary, but Vivian was implacable. She took his hand and led him forward with her most winning smile.

At last the girl seemed satisfied. She paused in a clearing beside an enormous rock, and asked Merlin if it had not been worth coming so far to find such a perfect place to rest at the end.

'This is certainly a very nice glade,' panted Merlin. 'But it is now quite dark, Vivian, and I can no longer see your pretty face so clearly.' He took the girl's hand and tried to gaze into her eyes. Vivian immediately jumped up and cried enthusiastically:

'Why, I am sure there is a cave behind this huge boulder, Merlin. We can explore! How romantic, I love caves.' Reluctantly the wizard got up once more and examined this boulder with her. He agreed that it was certainly a cave of sorts, but the boulder completely blocked the entrance. Vivian exclaimed petulantly that she wanted to see inside the cave, and refused to listen to all Merlin's pleas that they should leave the cave alone and sit down peacefully in the clearing. The more Merlin argued, the more Vivian tried to persuade him to use his magic to move the boulder.

'I don't believe you are a wizard after all,' cried the girl reproachfully. 'Look, a most beautiful flower is growing in that cave. Can you not see it, Merlin? Oh, I would grant anything to the brave man who plucked that flower for me.' Vivian had chosen her words well: the wizard was stung by the slight to his powers and thrilled by the thought of winning Vivian's favours. He replied boastfully that his magic was so strong that one word from him would move the boulder, or seal up the cave for all eternity.

'One word from you!' echoed Vivian in open admiration. 'Why, what a great sorcerer you are, Merlin. I never realized how powerful you were before. Supposing you told me that word, could I open or seal the cave too?' The wizard laughed confidently and told her that the word was so powerful that even a slip of a girl like Vivian could use it.

'Marvellous!' exclaimed Vivian. 'How clever you are, Merlin. To think that a mere girl like me could move that great boulder. Do let me try, dear Merlin.' She smiled up at the wizard like a spoilt child who is determined to get its own way. Merlin, poor infatuated old fool that he was, could not resist her appeal. Without stopping to reflect on the consequences of his rash action, he whispered the magic word in Vivian's ear.

'Now you are the sharer in my magic,' he said fondly. 'For armed with that spell, you are as powerful as Merlin himself and could imprison the wizard himself if you had the mind to do so.'

Vivian Reveals Herself in Her True Colours

Vivian's laugh tinkled sweetly in Merlin's ear, as if the very idea of imprisoning her protector was a ridiculous one.

'I must try out my new powers,' she declared, and forthwith, before Merlin could stop her, cried the magic word aloud. The boulder swung open and the cave yawned before them. Vivian pointed delightedly to a gorgeous purple flower growing in the depths of the cave.

'What did I say!' she exclaimed. 'You would have stopped me collecting the rarest flower in Britain if I hadn't insisted on your opening the cave, Merlin.' The wizard assured her that there was nothing he wanted more than to help her get the flower. Vivian clapped her hands.

'Oh, kind Merlin! Would you really go down into the cave and pluck the flower? I feel that once I get down there I shall never be able to climb back again.' Merlin replied gallantly that nothing would give him greater pleasure than to get the flower for Vivian; he was touched by the fact that she thought he was agile enough to climb down the chasm, and that she made no slighting reference to his age. Once he had offered, Vivian protested that it was too much to ask, but she allowed herself to be overruled. Feeling not a day older than twenty-five, Merlin threw away his stick and scrambled down the slope. The purple flower glowed at the far end of the cave. There was something sinister about its burning colour, and a faint sickly smell emanated from the bright green leaves. Merlin half-turned in doubt, to ask Vivian if she really wanted such a poisonous plant. Vivian thought he was turning back. Her pretty face contorted with triumph.

'Too late, old fool,' she hissed. The last thing Vivian saw, as the boulder rolled back in obedience to her magic command, was the expression of utter astonishment on Merlin's face. To the very end Merlin believed in the sweetness and innocence of the cruel sorceress who had lured him to his doom. So Merlin was immured in the cave by the spell which he himself had taught Vivian. No one knows how many hundred years he remained in his rocky prison, with nothing but bitter thoughts to keep him company. Some say that he is there still, lamenting the foolishness which led him into the trap which Morgan Le Fay had laid. But others think that centuries later God took pity on Merlin and remembered the many good deeds he had done in his lifetime, which were not all washed out by the silly infatuation at the end of his life. Then the boulder was rolled back by a knight in shining armour, and Merlin stepped forth – to be greeted by Sir Galahad himself, who had begged to be sent on this mission because it was Merlin who brought Lancelot to the convent and so helped Galahad find the Holy Grail. One can imagine the wonderful meeting which took place between Merlin and Galahad that day.

Whether that meeting ever took place or not, Merlin was now lost to the Knights of the Round Table for ever. King Arthur had lost a true friend and a valuable ally. He was now alone in the fight against Morgan Le Fay with no magic to support him. While Vivian and Morgan Le Fay rejoiced in the northern castle, the court of the Round Table waited in vain for the old man to return. When dawn came, and still he had not, Arthur sent out seach parties. A hundred knights combed the forest and dragged the lakes. No trace of Merlin or Vivian was ever found. The magic of Morgan Le Fay had taken good care to cover up their tracks. In time King Arthur came to believe that the aged wizard had fallen down some precipice with the girl, and he gave up his old friend for lost. How deeply then he regretted the coldness which had grown up between them during Merlin's last months at the court! Now he remembered only the wizard's kindness and thoughtfulness, the many times when he had saved Arthur from the consequences of his own rashness; the king thought back to his childhood, those far-off days with Merlin and Sir Hector. He mourned long for the old man.

Alas, although Arthur had heard the last of Merlin, he had not heard the last of Vivian.

14

MORDRED REBELS

A messenger came galloping towards Camelot on a sweating horse, beacons were lit on the Kentish hills, wild rumours were flying through Britain, and the news came to Arthur that the Norsemen had attacked the coast of Brittany in enormous numbers. An attack on Brittany meant that Britain itself was the next target. If the Norse succeeded in setting up a kingdom there, Arthur's kingdom would not remain long undisturbed. Arthur satisfied himself from the many reports which reached him that the Norse was going about the campaign in earnest: it was a major invasion which Brittany was facing, not simply a raid from a few greedy pirates. By this time the larger part of Britain had come beneath Arthur's overlordship. By good government and wise rule, Arthur had unified the south. But Arthur's power brought responsibility. When terrified women and children poured into the west from the eastern coast of Britain, because the flares of the men of the north shone out at them from the coast of France, it was time for action. Arthur sat in solemn council. He listened to the advice of his knights one by one.

'Leave the Bretons to fight their own battles,'

counselled Sir Bedevere, who was all for peace and plenty, and letting sleeping dogs lie.

'Are you thinking of your honour as a knight or your money bags as a wealthy landowner?' asked the king shrewdly, knowing Sir Bedevere's motives of old. The knight fell silent, abashed. Then Gawaine spoke up:

'We must think of the prosperity of our goodly kingdom, Sir Bedevere, not only of our private interests. Methinks that if the Norseman gain a hold on the coast of Brittany we shall never have another peaceful moment. Therefore I give my vote for going to the help of the Bretons.' King Arthur added approvingly: 'Well spoken, Gawaine. For you have taken more thought for the common weal than for your private profit. That was a worthy speech for a Knight of the Round Table. In addition, let us remember that Tristram of Cornwall, our noble vassal and former comrade, is a Breton by birth, and will surely go to the aid of his comrades. It behoves us to help him.'

It was generally felt that whatever the arguments against helping Brittany, they ought not to let Tristram down. When a final vote was taken, there was no dissentient voice. Now came the most difficult choice of Arthur's career. Who was he to leave behind to look after Britain, while he himself led the army against the Norsemen? It would not have occurred to Arthur, as it might to a modern leader, to stay at home himself, and send his best general into the fray.

Arthur's first impulse was to leave only Sir Bedevere behind, as in any case he was plainly reluctant to go. Then he reflected that trouble was anticipated up north and he could not trust Bedevere to leave his castle and make the long, difficult march north.

Having dismissed Bedevere, the obvious choice was Lancelot. Whoever stayed behind would have to look after the queen. Lancelot was the queen's knight, besides being the foremost champion at the court. No better person could have been imagined. But king or no king, Arthur was only human. Arthur was not exactly envious of Lancelot; but for so long Lancelot had outshone all the court in good looks, intelligence, and strength, that Arthur sometimes brooded on it. He sometimes wondered if people would have preferred to have Lancelot as king. Generally he was able to dismiss these thoughts as ridiculous. Lately, however, something had been happening which had stirred up his jealousy: Mordred had been dropping hints in the king's ear about Lancelot's relations with Gwenevere, which had gradually worn away Arthur's blind trust in the honour of his knight and his queen. Now Arthur did Lancelot a terrible injustice with these suspicions – for since the quest of the Holy Grail, Lancelot's love for Gwenevere had given way to the proper devotion of a knight to his queen. There had been a time when Arthur might have surprised looks of longing and passion passing between the two, but those days were long past. By the grace of God, the friendship of Gwenevere and Lancelot was without a trace of disloyalty to the king. But Arthur did not know this; he simply listened to Mordred's veiled allusions, and drew his own conclusions. In a fit of weakness, Arthur decided that Lancelot could not be trusted to govern Britain with Gwenevere. He concealed his real motives even from himself, by pretending that he needed Lancelot's strong right arm in the fight. But the fatal hint of jealousy was there all the same.

With Lancelot out of the question, the field was considerably narrowed. Sir Kay had not enough authority to undertake the task. Sir Gareth was too young. The only possible person left was Sir Gawaine, and as he had openly made a speech in favour of the common weal, he seemed a very good choice. But was Gawaine really capable of governing Britain all by himself? As Arthur knew, Gawaine was inclined to be moody, and also rather easily led. Arthur had, as he thought, a happy inspiration. He would leave Gawaine and Mordred together; these two had always got on well together, and indeed if Mordred had a fondness for anyone except himself, it was for Gawaine. So Arthur formally bestowed the governorship on Gawaine, with Mordred as his right-hand man. Then with a mighty flourish of trumpets, the host set off for France.

It was a brave sight! Helmets gleamed in the sun, the lances shone like a forest of steel. All the noble crests of Britain were to be seen on the shields. War-horses pawed the ground and snorted, in impatience to ride to battle and charge the enemy. Their rich trappings fluttered in the breeze, as the clank-clank of armour mingled with the clopping of hoofs, the cries of the knights, and the orders of the leaders, to make a confusion of rich sounds and a sight which had never been equalled at Camelot.

But what a tumult of rage and jealousy the unconscious Arthur left behind in the heart of Gawaine! It was one thing to make a public-spirited speech, and quite another to be asked to give up all the fun of the fight for the sober task of governing. The more Gawaine thought about it, the more shamefully he had been treated. He was an easy prey for Mordred. Egged on by Morgan Le Fay and Vivian, Mordred was full of tempting schemes.

'Fancy preferring Lancelot to you!' he would say, when the two knights were supposed to be in council about the government. 'Why, Gawaine, you could make yourself king of Britain in no time, if you had a mind, besides being the best fighter at court – and I *don't* mean next to Lancelot. The king must have been out of his mind to leave you behind. It would serve him right if you threw off his dominion.' Gawaine would smile deprecatingly at Mordred's praises and pretend that he thought these schemes were a joke. But both knew that Mordred was in deadly earnest.

Greatly daring, Mordred took Gawaine to the northern castle where dwelt his mother and Vivian. Gawaine was greatly surprised to discover that Vivian, whom everyone had supposed had perished with Merlin, was still alive. But before he had time to wonder more about it, Morgan Le Fay swept in and took his breath away with her beauty and enchantment. The years had not withered Morgan Le Fay, for had she not every magic spell at her command to keep her young and fair? Morgan Le Fay completed the process which Mordred had begun. While Mordred and Vivian made their own nefarious plans, Morgan Le Fay bewitched the wretched Gawaine. Gawaine's own wife grew pale and wan, as Gawaine's love for her faded, and he spent more and more time at the northern castle. In vain she reminded him of his duties as governor. Gawaine shook off her reproaches roughly and ordered her to keep her shrewish tongue off things which did not concern her.

King Arthur had been absent a month when Gawaine's general feelings of resentment were crystallized into determination to rebel. The four conspirators sat round Morgan Le Fay's table late at night and planned the revolt. The first step was obviously to imprison the Queen Gwenevere; and for this the most suitable prison was Gawaine's own castle. But when Vivian suggested that they should set fire to the Round Table, and so put an end to a loathsome tyranny, Gawaine started up in horror.

'Set fire to the Round Table! Never, while I live. Arthur may have behaved like a knave, but that does not exonerate me from my oath.'

'Vivian was only jesting,' replied Morgan Le Fay smoothly. She shot a look of hatred at the girl. This was not the first time some remark of Vivian's had endangered their plans. Morgan Le Fay began to wonder whether the girl had not outlived her usefulness now that Merlin was imprisoned. Besides, there was Mordred to be considered . . . and it would never do for the future king to become enamoured of a slut like Vivian.

'It seems the lady Vivian is weary,' continued Morgan Le Fay sweetly, 'and would be well advised to retire to her chamber.' There was no mistaking the command in the witch-queen's voice. Vivian said nothing. She looked first at Morgan Le Fay, and then at Mordred. Immediately Mordred fired up in her defence.

'Vivian is not a child,' he exclaimed angrily, 'to be sent up to bed. She has as good a head on her shoulders as anyone here.' Morgan Le Fay subjected Vivian to a long searching scrutiny. Her face was expressionless. At last she remarked:

'Yes, I see the lady Vivian is cleverer than I thought.' And there the matter rested. The planning of the rebellion continued without further incident. But the first rift in the conspirators had been made. In future Morgan Le Fay and Vivian would watch each other like jealous cats, and fight for the possession of Mordred.

It was decided to raise the standard of rebellion on Easter Sunday, a day on which a great crowd would be gathered in the cathedral of Camelot to celebrate the holy festival. Gawaine lined the aisles of the great building with his own men, armed to the teeth. As Arthur's nephew, he had wide lands and many retainers, all of whom were bound by their oath to support him in rebellion, whatever their private inclination. Also, Arthur had returned many of the lands which he had confiscated from the elder Mordred to the son, in an effort to win young Mordred's confidence. What with the soldiers whom Arthur had left behind for the governor, and the malcontents who are always glad to support a change of rule, Gawaine felt satisfied that he would be able to seize power without difficulty. He watched Gwenevere kneeling on a prie-dieu, slightly apart from the rest of the court as befitted her rank as queen. Her lovely face was impassive, and only her lips moved slightly as she prayed. The solemn High Mass drew to an end. The archbishop gave the blessing, and with incomparable dignity, Gwenevere rose to her feet and moved slowly down the aisle at the head of the courtiers. This was the signal for the revolt! As the queen passed, each soldier at the end of a pew rose to his feet and joined the procession. The clank of their mailed feet on the marble must have alarmed the queen; yet she did not turn her head, so well-trained was she in the ways of majesty.

Then, as Gwenevere came out on to the cathedral steps, Gawaine himself stepped forward and barred her way with his sword. Behind him stood Mordred. The queen drew herself up to her full height and said in a voice of authority:

'Sir Gawaine, let me pass. It is your queen who commands you.' Gawaine did not lower his sword. But some pang of shame and conscience must have struck him, for he could not meet the queen's eyes. He took refuge in bluster.

'You are no queen of mine!' he shouted, in a voice loud enough for all the crowd to hear. 'For your lord Arthur has played us all false. He has betrayed the kingdom to the Norsemen.' This was the story which Mordred had invented to satisfy the common people, who would otherwise never have gone over to the rebels, so well loved was Arthur. A great mumur went through the crowd. There were cries of 'Shame' and 'No, No' and 'False knight' and 'Betrayal', and private fights began to burst out between those who believed Gawaine and those who were prepared to defend Arthur to the death. All this time Gwenevere continued to gaze at Gawaine with such pain and reproach that Mordred himself must have been moved to pity had he dared meet her eyes.

At last she said in a low voice:

'Dear God, that I had not lived to see this grievous sight – a Knight of the Round Table betraying his oath.' But the die was cast now, and it was too late for Gawaine to turn back. He affected not to hear the queen's words, and drowned the tears of her women with a mighty shout.

'Arthur has deserted you! But Gawaine and Mordred are here to the rescue. Down with Arthur and long live Gawaine and Mordred, the champions of the people.' As if to challenge anyone who denied him, Gawaine brandished his sword in the air. While his men bore away

Gwenevere, Gawaine dominated the scene of tumult with his commanding presence. Mordred's men had covered the crowd so well, that every fellow who would have resisted this fearful treachery found himself cheek by jowl with an armed swordsman, ready to smite him down at the first word of resistance. Neverthless there were enough brave fellows to stand up for Arthur for a struggle to break out in front of the cathedral. Gawaine and Mordred flung themselves into the thick of the fray, Gawaine drowned his conscience in the bloodshed. Swords flashed in the sun that Easter morning, and blood ran on the holy stones. In vain the archbishop called to them to stop profaning the house of God. His feeble voice was drowned by the clash of steel and the cries of the dying. Many a goodly citizen met his death that day in the cause of Arthur, and many a villain too among Mordred's crew, got his deserts at the hand of one of Arthur's heroic champions. When Gawaine and Mordred at last got the upper hand – for they were many, and the defenders few – they had paid a high price for victory. All round the grey cathedral walls lay the wounded and the dying. The groans of the injured filled the air. Corpses were piled high against the cathedral itself. The reign of the usurpers had begun with bloodshed, and with bloodshed it was to continue.

For when the news of what Gawaine had done reached the outlying castles, there were many knights, stewards, and castellans, true to Arthur, who refused to acknowledge Gawaine's supremacy any longer. The seneschal of the Dark Tower, the most important outpost on the Welsh Frontier, sent a message of defiance to Camelot, and said that if Gawaine wanted his keys of office he could come and fetch them. Alas, his courage was not rewarded!

Forthwith Mordred got together a gang of ruffians who surrounded the gallant seneschal and battered down his tower. The seneshal sold his life dearly, taking a number of Mordred's cut-throats with him, but in the end superior numbers overwhelmed him. The Dark Tower fell into the hands of the usurpers, and its noble seneschal was buried in a nameless grave.

The news of the fall of the Dark Tower brought despair into the hearts of those who supported Arthur. How could they hope to stand out against Mordred and Gawaine, when they were so isolated, with no possibility of combining? It looked as if they were going to be wiped out one by one, and their castles burned about their heads. No leader came forward to head the resistance, for all the noblest knights were in France with the king, and the queen was immured in Gawaine's castle, and watched night and day by armed guards.

But such a reign of terror in the west of Britain could not hope to go unchecked. Two youths, whose father had been slain outside the cathedral of Camelot on Easter morning, achieved the perilous task of getting word to Arthur although the ports were guarded, and Gawaine's fleet patrolled the coast.

Their arrival was timely. For at the very moment at which these lads were disembarking, Arthur had just won a resounding victory over the Norsemen, and was planning to make for the south, and lead his Christian lances into the land of the Moors. Little knowing what dreadful news awaited him, he mused after his victory, and spun dreams for the future in which Spain, saved by the gallantry of the Round Table, would be Christian once more. The news that two messengers from Britain were waiting for an audience was exasperating. For the moment he did not particularly want to be recalled out of his day-dreams by the responsibilities of statecraft. But their terrible news jolted him immediately out of his lethargy.

'To arms, to arms!' cried Arthur. 'There is no time to lose! This very day we must be in Britain if we are not to lose our kingdom altogether. Oh false Gawaine, oh more than treacherous Mordred! Why did I ever trust you with the governorship!' The king smote his brow in anguish. 'Merlin!' he cried, 'if you can hear me now, harken to the laments of Arthur, who ignored your wise advice and now has to pay the penalty of his foolishness.' The king's distress was matched by Lancelot's: his heart ached at the thought of Gwenevere in captivity. No more news was known of the queen than that she had been imprisoned in Gawaine's castle and was being closely guarded, lest the loyalists should make an attempt to rescue her. Lancelot pictured her gazing listlessly from a turret window towards the coast of France, wondering whether each sail on the horizon might not be her husband and her champion hastening to deliver her.

He flung himself into the preparations for the departure, goading on the squires and himself gathering together the armour which had been cast carelessly aside after the battle. When the host finally stood ready to embark, it was largely by Lancelot's frantic efforts that such a quick assembly had been made. The heralds blew their trumpets, and the first war-horses were led aboard the boats, for the return to Britain. Gawaine's fleet was immediately on the alert. The ominous approach of large numbers of white sails cast the rebel navy into confusion.

Many of the sailors actually refused to fight against the king: loyalty was bred too strong in them, and they reasoned that since Arthur had apparently not deserted Britain, they had no cause to rebel. In vain the sea-captains cursed their crews, and tried to flog them into action. The cruel whips could not coerce the brave sailors who preferred to endure the lashes rather than lift a finger against their king. So determined was their mutiny that the captains were powerless. The sails flapped idly in the breeze while Gawaine's lieutenants raged on the decks.

Thus it was that Arthur's fleet sailed unharmed between the ranks of rebel ships, and was even greeted with cheers by the crews. The anguished king strode up the beach and demanded the latest news from the eager loyalists who had gathered to meet him. He learned that Gawaine and Mordred were at present encamped outside Gawaine's own castle, where they intended to hold a council of war and decide the best method of reducing the turbulent west, which so far resisted all their attempts to conquer it.

'A council of war!' exclaimed the king, in a cold fury. 'I will give them something to talk about. Forward, men, and don't rein your horses until we have confronted the traitors face to face.' With the famous war-cry, known of old in many a noble battle, Arthur gave the signal for the advance. Then his mighty army galloped on towards the castle of Gawaine. After Arthur rode Sir Lancelot, second to none in splendour, with his horse's mane flowing in the wind, and the proud plume of his helmet waving gaily above his head. After him, Sir Gareth, who had won a great reputation in France, Sir Bedevere, on a fine charger, Sir Kay, who was never far from the front rank,

Geraint of Devon, who had left Devon to join the king against the Norsemen, Tristram, who had abandoned Cornwall at Arthur's call, and many others whose adventures would fill a score of books. In each heart burnt rage against the traitors, and determination to avenge the insult which had been dealt the king, with death. Each knight desired to be the one who struck down Mordred with his own hand: for it was significant that the Knights of the Round Table had no hesitation in ascribing the chief blame to Mordred. Unlike Arthur, many of them had discerned the evil thoughts which lay beneath Mordred's smiling face. They knew Gawaine to be impulsive and easily roused; the wiser of the knights guessed that Mordred had played upon Gawaine's fiery temper and persuaded him into a rebellion which he was probably even now regretting. Lancelot alone refused to make any excuses for Gawaine; the news that the queen had been seized outside the cathedral and borne roughly to Gawaine's castle incensed him. He would allow nothing to be said in extenuation of Gawaine's treachery.

'God grant me the chance to strike him down like the dog he is!' was all Lancelot would say when Gawaine's name was mentioned.

The noise of this great host approaching reached the ears of the rebels long before the first horseman could be distinguished. The ground shook beneath their thundering hoofs. The faint shout of their war-cries was borne on the air to the ears of Gawaine and Mordred as they sat in council. What pang of conscience and regret gripped the heart of Gawaine then? He turned pale and muttered a prayer. Mordred watched him cynically and laughed.

'Too late for prayers now, my friend,' he said at length. 'Unless you are enlisting the help of the devil.'

'He would be a worthy patron for our cause,' said Gawaine, half under his breath. Mordred, who read the signs of Gawaine's change of heart, pretended not to notice. He continued to make plans for conquering Britain, as if victory were certain. When Gawaine suggested tentatively that they might make a treaty with Arthur, dividing the realm amicably between them, Mordred laughed him to scorn:

'A treaty with Arthur Pendragon! Why, Gawaine, where are your oaths of defiance now? Did you not vow to take all his dominions from him, in revenge for the insults he put upon you? Besides, Arthur would never consent to divide what he once ruled alone.' The last remark was a shrewd blow and Gawaine knew it. The die had been cast on Easter Day, and there was no turning back now. Gawaine flung himself into the task of defeating his king. If a pitched battle it was to be, then Gawaine would do his utmost to win; and if he was killed in the attempt, well, perhaps in his secret heart, the knight thought that was the best solution of all.

But Gawaine was not to be given the satisfaction of losing himself in the mêlée of a battle. Arthur drew up his soldiers on a moor a league or so from the castle, from which their lances glinted ominously in the eyes of Gawaine's own soldiers, encamped outside the castle walls. The sun shone brightly in spite of stormy clouds, but Gawaine shivered as he mounted the battlements with Mordred and surveyed the two armies drawn up opposite each other.

'I have a feeling that I shall not live to see that sun go

down,' he said slowly to his companion. Mordred glanced at Gawaine's brooding face, and something like remorse overcame him for a moment. If there was any human being Mordred really loved, it was Gawaine; and for a single second Mordred regretted the evil net which he had woven round his friend. Then he steeled himself to remark cheerfully:

'When the sun goes down we shall be kings, not knights.'

Sir Lancelot Sends a Challenge

But what was this trumpeter doing, leaving the ranks of Arthur and making his way on foot to the opposing army? The fellow flew a white flag from his trumpet. Could Arthur be suing for peace already? Mordred could not believe his eyes. But thoughts of peace were as far from the king's mind as from Mordred's. The trumpeter bore a challenge from Lancelot to Gawaine.

'Traitor knight!' it ran, 'come forth and show yourself. Do not lurk in your castle, but ride out and give battle to the noble knight, Sir Lancelot, who challenges you. If Sir Lancelot defeats you, it is your duty to release the Queen Gwenevere from imprisonment.'

Gawaine's blood boiled at Lancelot's challenge: here was a chance to match his skill against his rival and prove himself the better man. Years of envy for Lancelot rose up in Gawaine's memory and he vowed to give the queen's champion such a drubbing that he would never dare show his face in Britain again. Mordred rejoiced to see that his friend had recovered his composure. He agreed to release Gwenevere in the unlikely chance of Lancelot winning the battle. Gawaine girded himself for the fight, whistling cheerfully at the prospect of avenging ancient wrongs. In the opposite camp Lancelot knelt in prayer and begged that he might release Gwenevere from odious captivity if it was the last thing he did on earth.

So the two champions rode out against each other. A magnificent sight in one way – two men in the prime of life mounted on splendid chargers: but in another sense the saddest sight in Britain. For the unity of the Round Table was broken, and for the first time two knights were fighting against each other, instead of side by side. Arthur could not hide his grief at the sight: he retired into his tent, and sat with his face buried in his hands, not knowing how to endure this terrible grief at the collapse of his life's work.

A FIGHT TO THE DEATH

The champions paced their steeds warily up and down, holding them on a tight rein, while they eyed each other. The opposing armies were silent. In the vast expectant hush, only the clink of armour could be heard, and the neighing of Lancelot's war-horse which suddenly reared up and pawed with its gigantic hoofs wildly in the air. Gawaine seized his chance. Spurring his own mount, he aimed for Lancelot at a gallop. The knight had only just time to control his horse, when Gawaine was upon him with the ferocious thrust of his lance. Shaken by the horse's fit of temper, Lancelot could only put his shield between Gawaine's onslaught and his body. The iron shield, emblazoned with Lancelot's crest, buckled under the blow. With an oath Lancelot threw away the useless weapon. He was now unprotected against Gawaine's attacks. His only strength lay in an attack so violent that all Gawaine's energies would be occupied in defending himself. Lancelot wheeled his horse, and made for Gawaine: he thrust at the traitor with such force that a lesser man would have fallen to the ground at the first impact of the blow. But Gawaine, practised in many tournaments, was wily enough to let the blow glance off his shoulder, and return to the attack with vigour.

Grievous as it was, this was surely the finest battle which had ever been seen in Britain! Back and forth went the two champions, neither conceding an inch, yet Lancelot all the time with the fearful disadvantage of having lost his shield. It was this which would decide the day, thought Gwenevere sadly as she watched, for no man could survive very long in such a fierce fight without a shield. She reckoned without Lancelot. He summoned all the tricks he knew to keep off Gawaine, and turned the loss of his shield into a positive advantage, by using his unencumbered arm to control his horse with incredible agility.

A hundred times Lancelot seemed lost, and a hundred times Gawaine seemed about to fall. At last Sir Lancelot succeeded in making Gawaine lose his balance in earnest; but the champion did not topple from his horse – instead he leapt to the ground and challenged Lancelot to meet him there with his sword. Springing from the saddle, Lancelot rushed at him with brandished blade, and the two engaged in savage hand-to-hand combat. Who knows what extra ounce of skill gave Lancelot the advantage – or was it Gawaine's evil conscience which held him back from securing the ultimate victory? For suddenly

Gawaine seemed to falter. Lancelot was on him in a flash, cutting and thrusting like the great swordsman he was. In vain Gawaine defended himself, and exerted all his strength to hold off the ferocious onslaught. Lancelot was fighting for the queen and the cause which he believed in. His strength was as the strength of ten. With a final sweeping blow he penetrated Gawaine's mail and pierced him through and through. As the two armies held their breath, the knight crumpled up and fell upon the ground.

As he lay there his glazed eyes met those of Lancelot.

'Forgive me, Lancelot,' he gasped out. Lancelot fell on his knees beside him, and tried to staunch the fearful wound.

'Alack, Gawaine,' cried Lancelot in agony, 'would that I had not lived to see this day when two knights of the Round Table fought each other. Forgive me, forgive me, Gawaine, for the fell deed to which my loyalty drove me.' The dying knight rallied himself enough to grasp Lancelot's hand and whisper in an ever-fading voice:

'All . . . my . . . fault . . . I . . . repent . . . me of what I have done.' Then he cried in a strong voice, 'Let there be no more bloodshed,' and fell back lifeless on the turf. A deep murmur went up from both camps. Whatever his weaknesses, Gawaine had been well loved on both sides, and there was not one dry eye among all the thousands of soldiers assembled there, as they saw the noble champion breathe his last. King Arthur wept openly to think that so gallant a knight had died a traitor's death, and Lancelot was beside himself with grief.

Within the castle itself, Mordred faced his mother, Morgan Le Fay, with a white face in which fury and desperate grief were mixed.

'This is your work, witch,' he spat at her, not caring how the tears rolled down his cheeks. 'But for your evil counsel, a gallant knight would not have died this day. He was the only true friend I had, and you have killed him by your cursed magic! Oh would that God had given me a woman for a mother instead of a witch!' At these harsh words from her son, Morgan Le Fay's heart felt as if it would crack across with pain at his injustice. It was for Mordred that she had woven her plots and employed her spells: she had planned all these years to defeat Arthur, purely in order to place Mordred on the throne.

'Get you from my sight,' commanded Mordred in an icy voice. 'Begone, witch, and never show your face before me again, else I will have you slain for the sorceress you are.' For a second Morgan Le Fay could scarcely take in the import of his words. She stood before him as if stunned. Then she sprang at Vivian's throat, screaming:

'This is your doing, slut! You have turned my son against his mother! May the devil himself give me strength to tear out your black heart from your breast.' It took all Mordred's strength to pull off the maniacal woman from her victim. Even when he had disengaged her, she still made desperate attempts to claw and scratch Vivian with her long nails: she crouched there, heaving and sobbing with humiliation and fury.

Contemptuously Mordred dragged Morgan Le Fay from the room, and half guided her, half pushed her down the turret stairs. He did not even look back over his shoulder to see what had become of the woman who was his mother.

'Vivian!' he exclaimed, 'you and I at least shall repent of our evil ways and make peace with Arthur. Together we will try and wipe out the evil name which I have won. We shall spend the rest of our lives atoning for the death of the noble Gawaine, by self-sacrifice and service.'

Vivian cast down her eyes as if in repentance.

'It shall be as my lord Mordred says,' she replied. There was no expression in her voice.

Forthwith, Mordred rode to the head of the army which was now his alone, and ordered ambassadors of peace to go to Arthur's camp, where they would sue for pardon. He watched his emissaries enter the royal tent from his vantage point. In a short time they were riding back with the glad news that Arthur had accepted Mordred's professions of sorrow and would receive the leader himself in person.

The noonday sun flashed down on the two mighty ranks as they stood in silence, drawn up on the moor. How many soldiers then breathed a prayer of gratitude for Gawaine's death which, far from being in vain, had saved thousands from death! One soldier, at least, resolved to kneel down in prayer. Stepping backward sharply, his mailed foot came down on the head of a sleeping adder, basking peacefully in the warmth. The enraged snake flew up at him. The fellow drew his sword from its sheath and slew the poisonous reptile with a quick cut of his blade this way and that. What evil chance directed Vivian's gaze to one soldier among so many? For behold, as the flashing blade caught the sun, Vivian drew at Mordred's sleeve and exclaimed:

'My lord, my lord, we are betrayed! The soldiers of Arthur have drawn their swords on us!' No sooner had Mordred too seen the flashing blade, than all his good resolutions vanished. Shouting 'We are betrayed! We are betrayed!' he waved his sword in the air and urged his troops into the fatal charge which began the greatest battle ever seen in Britain. Arthur lost no time in meeting this unexpected attack. He too waved his sword in the air and gave the signal for the assault.

From her knoll Vivian watched her work, well pleased, with a smile of satisfaction on her cruel lips.

15

BATTLE ROYAL

A hundred years later, this battle was still remembered in
Britain as the fiercest which had ever raged in the land: for
each man fought to the death and sold his life as dearly as
he could. All day long the battle raged: now one side
seemed to be winning, and now the other; yet by sunset,
when the last red rays of the sun were staining the grey
walls of Gawaine's castle, you still could not say definitely
that either party had the advantage.

There had not been time for either army to work out a
plan of battle, so impulsive had been the beginning of the
struggle. Mordred had simply urged his men to the attack
and Arthur followed suit. Thus the battlefield divided
itself into a number of private combats, in which the
soldiers worked off old scores against their enemies. Brave
Sir Gareth was one of the first to fall – at the hand of a
burly squire who had long envied him his royal estate, and
desired to lower him from his high position. Indeed
Gareth never would have fallen, if it had not been for the
superior odds against him. Single-handed he would have
held off this squire for ever, for Gareth was second to none
in valour. But the squire could not even abide by the most
elementary rule of chivalry and settle his score alone. As

Gareth pressed the squire back into a clump of scrubby bushes, and would have forced him to yield at the point of the sword, the squire shouted for help at the top of his craven voice. Alas, his cowardice was the means of the gallant Gareth's destruction. Half a dozen knaves rushed up and bore the lone knight to the ground. He drew his last breath on earth with seven sword wounds in his body – for all its sadness, a noble death, because Gareth had not flinched from the fight in spite of the terrible odds against him.

Tristram of Cornwall was responsible for the deaths of a great regiment of traitors before he too succumbed to his wounds, and was borne by his faithful squires to die in the arms of his lady Iseult, who waited near by in the royal tent, weeping and praying with the Queen Gwenevere.

'Be of good heart, my queen,' gasped Tristram to Iseult. 'What better death can a man die, than in the arms of his beloved wife, as the result of wounds bravely sustained in battle. Fear not, Iseult, the forces of good will never be defeated in Britain.' As Iseult felt Tristram's hands grow icy to her touch, she fell back into the arms of her women with one single cry of anguish.

In the thickest of the fight were to be found Arthur and Lancelot, striking out side by side like the lifelong comrades that they were. In vain Lancelot urged the king to save himself, when the tide of battle seemed to be turning against them. Arthur refused to spare himself anything which he could not spare the least of his soldiers. All day long he sought Mordred among the foe, burning to slay the traitor with his own hand, and so avenge the broken peace of Britain. But Mordred eluded him. Wherever the fight was thickest, there was Mordred in the midst of it, laying about him vigorously; but when the king espied him, Mordred vanished to the farthest quarter of the conflict. It was as if Mordred feared to meet his king face to face, equally unwilling to slay or be slain by him.

So the tumultuous hours passed. Sir Kay died valiantly defending Arthur, true to the last to the fidelity which had inspired him since their boyhood together. Geraint of Devon threw himself in front of the queen's tent, and staved off her recapture by his body across the threshold. It was Geraint's valiant death which drew Lancelot's attention to the queen's peril. This drew him away from Arthur's side at last; summoning the remainder of his men-at-arms, he made his way to the royal tent, prepared to defend it or die in the attempt.

Not all the fights which took place that day were held between knight and knight; for as evening came Morgan Le Fay crept back on to the field of battle, determined to find Vivian and avenge her humiliation at the girl's hand. As Vivian watched the fray from a small hill, the witch-queen glided up to her and plunged her gilded dagger deep into that cruel heart. Vivian died with the cold smile still upon her lips. Her graceful figure slumped forward and fell in a heap at the witch-queen's feet.

'So perish all who thwart my designs!' cried Morgan Le Fay aloud.

'Not so fast!' exclaimed a loud voice behind her. Turning, Morgan Le Fay found herself face to face with an avenger in the shape of her son Mordred. She cowered back and sought to hide her face from his angry gaze. But he would have none of that and tore back the veils from her face, so that she might see the full extent of his scorn and hatred.

'I warned you not to come before me again,' said Mordred between gritted teeth. 'You brought about the destruction of my friend. Now you have stabbed the girl I loved with your own hands. This time your crime shall not pass unpunished. As she died, so shall you!' So saying, Mordred bent down to the corpse of Vivian, and plucked out the gilded dagger from her breast.

'Gawaine and Vivian! Your deaths are avenged.' With these words Mordred plunged the dagger into the heart of Morgan Le Fay. Without even waiting to witness her death, he returned to the scene of the battle. Thus did Morgan Le Fay meet the death which she richly deserved, at the hands of her own son.

When evening came, the flower of the Round Table lay dead upon the field. Of the champions, only Lancelot and Arthur remained on one side, and Mordred on the other. Percival had died as he lived, sacrificing himself for others. Seeing that his squire was without a sword, having lost his in the scrimmage, Percival gave his own blade to the boy, and defended himself with his dagger. The puny weapon could not long survive the onslaughts of the rebels on all sides. Percival fell beneath a rain of blows, with scarcely time to whisper a last prayer for forgiveness for the many deaths he had caused that day.

Yet still the battle raged, all the fiercer for the depleted numbers. Each man now felt it his duty to fight as ten. Round the queen's tent raged the most bitter fight, for there Lancelot continually rallied his men to fresh feats of courage for the sake of their queen. One by one his faithful henchmen fell to the ground and rose no more. And still the attackers came on with undiminished vigour, for they had the advantage of numbers, and still had reserves to call upon. At last only Lancelot faced the oncoming hordes. His mighty figure on the blood-stained threshold of the tent daunted the first ranks of the attackers. But gradually they took courage from the fact that he was one, and they were many. Lancelot found himself facing attack on all sides. Pausing only to shout to the queen:

'Fly, Gwenevere, fly while there is still time! For the sake of our love, save yourself, that you may live to tell the tale of this sad day,' Sir Lancelot turned to face the greatest and the last fight of his life. In anguish Gwenevere harkened to his words, and motioned to Iseult and Enid to follow her, as she made her way across the sodden field of battle, to a nearby convent and safety. It cost Gwenevere all her training as a queen to desert Lancelot in his hour of peril. But her reason told her that if Arthur conquered, she would see Lancelot again. Whereas if Mordred held the day, it would be well for one witness to the glories of the Round Table to survive into the new godless Britain. So Gwenevere went, with many a backward glance to the staunch figure of her lover, covering her retreat. The last she saw of him, he was nearly overwhelmed by the scores of his attackers, yet still kept his feet and uttered mighty war-cries which rang out across the moor.

At length these cries ceased, and only the clash of swords was heard. Scarcely daring to turn her head, Gwenevere cast one more backward glance. Then her heart seemed to stop beating. For Lancelot was no longer to be seen, and where his mighty figure had stood, there was now nothing except a scrum of rebels, rejoicing horribly.

Caring not what became of her, Gwenevere left the side of Iseult, and rushed blindly back into the fight. Even the traitors gave way before her wild and grief-stricken figure. They parted to allow her to see the body of Lancelot, stretched forth on the ground. With a terrible cry, Gwenevere lifted up his head. Their eyes met in one long, last gaze.

'For ever and for ever,' gasped Lancelot. He could say no more. His eyes glazed, and his head sagged forward, lifeless. The rebels melted back into the fight, and Gwenevere was left alone with the dead body of her champion. An hour she rested there. Then she stopped a passing squire she recognized from the old days at Camelot, and persuaded him to bear Lancelot's body to the convent. There Gwenevere kept a lonely vigil in the chapel beside the coffin. Who shall tell what thoughts were hers in that desolate hour?

Meanwhile, Arthur fought on, hardly caring whether he was victorious or not, now that all his gallant knights had perished. It was enough for him to slay the traitor Mordred, and then he would die content. In the ground in front of the castle, the two at last came face to face.

'Now prepare to meet your death, Mordred!' cried Arthur, whirling his sword above his head.

'Arthur Pendragon,' replied Mordred, 'your last hour has come.' Then they charged. Arthur's horse was weary, and Mordred's no less. Yet the bitter determination of the two men seemed to have communicated itself to the two horses. For they summoned all their flagging energy to bear their respective masters to the assault. Yet Mordred was no match for Arthur. Mordred was many years younger than the king, but not for nothing had Arthur led the most formidable fighting force in Europe into battle for twenty years and more. The presence of Mordred whipped Arthur into a final display of strength and skill which he never equalled even in the days of his youth. Raising his arm to its full height, Arthur charged Mordred, and thrust his lance right through the joints of his armour.

Mordred quivered at the impact, like a target transfixed by an arrow. He tumbled from his horse, with the lance still sticking in his breast, and swayed before Arthur on one knee. The king dismounted. He expected some show of repentance from the traitor on the point of death. One can only guess the desperate thoughts which passed through Mordred's head at that moment. Forcing himself up the length of the lance, he smote the king a dreadful blow with his sword.

No man could survive long with a lance piercing him through and through. Mordred fell heavily to the ground.

'I have killed him,' whispered Arthur, 'but I fear that he has killed me.' So saying, he tumbled back into the arms of the faithful Sir Bedevere, with the blood flowing freely from the deep wound which Mordred had dealt him.

The death of Mordred had turned the tide of battle. The rebels now lost heart and fled. The king's champions, few though they were, found themselves in possession of the field. The tattered royal standard fluttered from the flagpost of Gawaine's castle; and to the fortress was borne Arthur on a litter, while the best leeches in the kingdom tried to stem his life's blood from flowing away. Arthur listened to the reports of victory in silence. He could not conceal his grief as the news of the death of knight after knight was brought to him.

'We have paid a heavy price,' he murmured to Sir Bedevere. 'God grant that those who come after me will consider it worth it.'

'Do not speak of your successors, my liege,' replied Bedevere loyally. 'For me, there will never be any king but Arthur.' The king roused himself on his pillows and said hoarsely:

'No, Bedevere, the hour of my death is nigh. We both know that Mordred dealt me my death-blow. You must help the new king to govern the kingdom as I would have wished. It is your duty, good Sir Bedevere. Do not shrink from it.'

'As my liege commands,' replied Sir Bedevere, kneeling and kissing Arthur's hand. The king sank back satisfied. An hour later he stirred again.

'Bedevere,' he said weakly, 'the time has come. Take me on your back and carry me to the lake where I found Excalibur.' At first the knight thought Arthur had left his senses. But the king insisted, and Bedevere had to obey him. Reluctantly he strapped Excalibur to the king's side, and took him on his back. Now Arthur pointed to the right, now to the left, but his weak voice never faltered in its directions. The way which had proved so tortuous all those years ago with Merlin, now seemed simple.

It was not long before Bedevere found himself in the deserted woods which surrounded the lonely lake. The scene had not changed since Arthur last gazed at the thick reeds and dark, still waters. But now no boat lurked among the rushes. There was no sign of life at all. Arthur bade Bedevere lay him down among the trees and ungird Excalibur.

'I am too weak, Bedevere,' he whispered. 'Take Excalibur and hurl the great sword far into the lake. Then come back and tell me what you saw.' Bedevere took Excalibur and examined the famous blade. He saw the

two messages, 'Keep me' and 'Cast me away', orna-
mented with rich jewels on either side. But when Bedevere
reached the side of the lake, and made as if to hurl the
sword into it, the demon of covetousness whispered in his
ear – 'Why waste a good sword like this? Why not keep
Excalibur and fight on for Arthur after his death with the
king's own sword?'

Persuading himself that his motives were really very
pure, Bedevere went back to the king and told him that he
had cast Excalibur into the lake.

'And what saw you then?' demanded Arthur anxiously.
Bedevere drew upon his imagination.

'I saw the wind stir the rushes round the lake,' he said.
'And a flight of wild geese sprang up from the sedge.'

'Liar!' bellowed Arthur in something like his old voice.
'Go back, Bedevere, and do as I bade you.' Disconsolately
Bedevere went back to the lake and took the sword from its
hiding-place among the rushes. Once more he admired
the workmanship of the blade. Once more greed was too
much for honour. Hastily Bedevere restored Excalibur to
its hiding-place, and returned to the king.

'This time what did you see?' asked Arthur. He spoke
with difficulty.

'A marvellous sight,' reported Bedevere eagerly. 'One
of the wild geese circled thrice round the sword and bore it
away in its beak.' Bedevere was rather proud of this flight
of imagination, which he thought should satisfy the king.
But a second time Arthur shouted at him 'Liar!' although
his voice was noticeably weaker.

Bedevere retraced his steps to the lake a third time. A
third time he balanced Excalibur in his hands. But this
time his loyalty to Arthur outweighed his greed.

Suppressing a sigh of regret, he whirled the famous sword once round his head, and cast it far into the lake, as far as his strength would take it. Then, before Bedevere's amazed eyes, the waters of the still lake parted, and a hand, clothed in a white sleeve, issued out of the bosom of the lake. Straight as a die, Excalibur sped to the waiting hand. The jewels of the hilt glinted before Bedevere's eyes. It was the last he ever saw of Excalibur. The hand sank slowly below the waters, until not even the tip of the sword was visible. So calm was the surface of the lake, that Bedevere wondered if he had not dreamed the whole incident.

He returned a third time to Arthur. This time he did not wait to be asked.

'I saw a white arm issue forth from the bosom of the lake,' he said, 'and grasp the good sword Excalibur. Then both hand and sword sank below the waters, until no trace of them remained.'

'It is good,' said Arthur contentedly. 'The Lady of the Lake has reclaimed her own. The time has come for me to die.' As he spoke, Bedevere saw a black boat steal across the lake, in which sat six ladies clothed all in black. Beneath their dark veils glinted crowns of strange antique design. At a sign from Arthur, Bedevere carried the king to the edge of the lake. From there the six queens bore him on into the boat, speaking not a word to either the knight or the king. Before Bedevere's grief-stricken eyes, the king was carried away across the lake until the evening mists hid him from the knight's gaze. Bedevere was left alone on the shore, feeling as if his heart had been borne away across the lake with the body of his king.

'I must go back to Camelot and set about the task of

restoring order, which Arthur laid upon me,' said the knight sadly. Turning his heel, he looked once more across the waters, in the direction in which Arthur had disappeared. Then he made his way slowly back through the desolate forests.

So none actually saw Arthur's death. From this fact springs the legend that Arthur is not really dead, but will come back again when Britain is in need, to save his beloved country. Whether Arthur was dead or not, the good that he had done lived after him. By the efforts of Gwenevere and Bedevere, and the Knights of the Round Table who were left, peace was restored in Britain, for Arthur had given an example of leadership and courage which was never to be forgotten.

Since then, the stories of his knights and his court have been told and retold down the centuries. The exploits of Lancelot and the other champions have become legends, and Arthur himself has achieved the fame which he vowed to win. Today, over a thousand years later, we feel proud to remember that King Arthur and the Knights of the Round Table are part of our national heritage.